Life in the Pouch

Life in the Pouch

Kangaroo Parenting Secrets

Maria M

Spectra Enterprise

CONTENTS

INDEX

INTRODUCTION

The kangaroo, a notable image of Australia, has long caught the world's creative mind with its one of a kind regenerative system and particular nurturing techniques. Among marsupials, kangaroos stand apart for their pocket based way to deal with supporting their young, known as joeys. Life in the pocket is a surprising excursion that discloses the mysteries of kangaroo nurturing — a many-sided dance of science, transformation, and endurance.

In this far reaching investigation, we dig into the profundities of kangaroo nurturing, disentangling the secrets disguised inside the pocket. From the marvelous birth of a small, lacking joey to the mind boggling phases of pocket life and the inevitable progress to freedom, kangaroo nurturing is a demonstration of the strength and flexibility of these marsupials. As we set out on this excursion, we try to reveal the secret subtleties, organic wonders, and transformative systems that characterize life in the pocket for kangaroos.

1. **A Wonder of Marsupial Multiplication:**
   The tale of kangaroo nurturing starts with a wonder of marsupial generation. Dissimilar to placental well evolved creatures, kangaroos bring forth exceptionally lacking youthful after a short incubation period. The little joey, weighing simply a negligible portion of a gram, sets out on an excursion from the birth channel to the mother's pocket, directed by a mix of nature and maternal help. The multifaceted subtleties of this birthing system set up for the exceptional nurturing adventure that unfurls inside the limits of the pocket.

2. **Pocket Life: A Safe-haven of Development and Improvement:**
   The pocket, a particular component of marsupials, fills in as a safe-haven where the joey goes through momentous development and improvement. Inside this warm and defensive climate, the joey connects itself to a nipple, where it gets sustenance and encounters the beginning phases of life. We investigate the

progressive phases inside the pocket, from the weak early days to the snapshots of arising interest as the joey develops further and stronger.

3. **Maternal Consideration: The Heartbeat of Kangaroo Nurturing:**
At the center of kangaroo nurturing is the unmatched maternal consideration given by the mother kangaroo. The close connection among mother and joey is manufactured through a progression of ways of behaving, including prepping, licking, and steady vicinity. The musical heartbeat of the mother turns into a consoling presence for the joey, reflecting the perplexing dance of science and feeling that characterizes the kangaroo nurturing experience.

4. **The Progress to Freedom:**
Life in the pocket is a transient stage, and the possible progress to freedom is an essential second in a kangaroo's life. We unwind the slow cycle by which joeys rise out of the pocket, gain strength and coordination, and start to investigate the outer world. The difficulties and wins of this change grandstand the versatility and flexibility imbued in kangaroo nurturing.

5. **Social Elements inside the Crowd:**
Kangaroos are not single animals; they flourish in gatherings known as crowds. Inside the crowd, social elements assume a vital part in the childhood of joeys. We dive into the associations between kangaroos, investigating the jobs of more seasoned kin, the foundation of orders, and the mind boggling correspondence frameworks that add to the attachment of the kangaroo local area.

6. **Difficulties and Variations:**
Life in the pocket and past isn't without its difficulties. Kangaroos should explore natural tensions, hunter dangers, and the steadily changing scene of the Australian outback. We investigate the striking variations and methods for surviving utilized by kangaroos, from their strong rear leg kicks to their capacity to identify and answer expected risks.

7. **Human-Untamed life Associations:**
As human exercises infringe on normal natural surroundings, kangaroos should adjust to a world progressively molded by human presence. We analyze the intricacies of human-natural life associations, including the difficulties presented by urbanization, environment fracture, and protection endeavors pointed toward adjusting the necessities of kangaroos with those of human networks.

8. **Protection Goals:**
Kangaroos, as necessary parts of Australia's environments, face protection challenges in a quickly impacting world. We investigate the protection goals, including territory safeguarding, supportable administration rehearses, and the requirement for public attention to guarantee the endurance of kangaroo populaces and the environmental equilibrium they add to.

9. **Social Importance and Imagery:**
Past their natural significance, kangaroos hold social importance in Native

Australian people group and act as public images. We dig into the Dreamtime stories, craftsmanship, and customary practices that commend the kangaroo's part in Native legacy. Moreover, we investigate how kangaroos have become significant of Australia, highlighting noticeably in its social personality and worldwide acknowledgment.

10. **Logical Experiences and Mechanical Headways:**

Kangaroo nurturing has been a subject of logical interest, prompting mechanical headways in research. We investigate the instruments and strategies, including GPS following, satellite symbolism, and hereditary examination, that have empowered researchers to unwind the secrets of kangaroo conduct. The logical bits of knowledge acquired from concentrating on kangaroos contribute not exclusively to how we might interpret marsupial science yet additionally to more extensive conversations in similar science and nature.

In this broad investigation of life in the pocket and the mysteries of kangaroo nurturing, we leave on an excursion that rises above science to envelop culture, preservation, and logical request. As we uncover the complexities of kangaroo nurturing, we gain a significant appreciation for the wonders of marsupial life, the flexibility of these famous animals, and the sensitive equilibrium expected for their endurance in the consistently developing scenes they call home.

1. **Overview of Kangaroo Parenting**

Kangaroos, with their famous bouncing step and unmistakable pockets, exemplify the remarkable universe of marsupials, exhibiting an exceptional way to deal with nurturing that has enthralled researchers and nature lovers the same. This exhaustive outline dives into the unpredictable embroidery of kangaroo nurturing, investigating the wonders of marsupial proliferation, the supporting climate of the pocket, maternal consideration elements, and the versatile step by step processes for surviving that characterize the existences of these notable Australian marsupials.

1. **Marsupial Propagation: An Extraordinary Natural Wonder:**
Correlations with Placental Well evolved creatures:
The excursion of kangaroo nurturing starts with an investigation of marsupial propagation, an unmistakable takeoff from the conceptive techniques of placental well evolved creatures. A short development period comes full circle in the introduction of profoundly lacking youthful, making way for the wonderful change from the birth trench to the pocket.
Birth and the Excursion to the Pocket:
The introduction of a kangaroo joey is a demonstration of the wonders of marsupial proliferation. We dig into the complexities of this cycle, from the

weak snapshot of birth to the joey's astounding excursion, directed by intuition and maternal help, to the security of the mother's pocket. The physical and conduct variations expected for this excursion feature the uniqueness of kangaroo proliferation.

2. **The Pocket as a Safe-haven for Development and Improvement:**
Life structures and Capability of the Pocket:

The pocket, a sign of marsupial life structures, fills in as a defensive climate where joeys go through critical development and improvement. We investigate the physical elements of the pocket, including solid design and the nipples give fundamental sustenance to the creating joey. The pocket's job as a safe-haven for early improvement becomes obvious as we disentangle the phases of pocket life.

Phases of Pocket Life:

Life inside the pocket is an excursion set apart by particular transformative phases. From the weak long stretches of outset to the continuous rise of a stronger joey, each stage is a demonstration of the multifaceted interaction of natural cycles. We analyze the development achievements, tactile encounters, and maternal communications that shape the joey's initial life inside the pocket.

3. **Maternal Consideration: The Heartbeat of Kangaroo Nurturing:**
Close Connection Among Mother and Joey:

Fundamental to the outcome of kangaroo nurturing is the personal connection among mother and joey. Maternal consideration goes past the arrangement of sustenance; it envelops prepping, licking, and consistent nearness. We investigate the close to home and social parts of this bond, revealing insight into the heartbeat of kangaroo nurturing.

Correspondence and Social Elements:

Kangaroos, known for their social designs, take part in a complex type of correspondence. Inside the setting of nurturing, correspondence among mother and joey assumes a vital part in encouraging a feeling of safety and understanding. We unwind the nuanced vocalizations, non-verbal communication, and material prompts that work with correspondence inside the kangaroo family.

4. **The Change to Autonomy:**
Continuous Investigation of the Outside Climate:

The change from pocket to freedom is an achievement in kangaroo nurturing. As joeys gain strength and coordination, they continuously investigate the outside climate. We look at the movement abilities, tangible turn of events, and social variations that describe this essential period of freedom.

Social Elements Past the Pocket:

Kangaroos are social creatures that flourish in gatherings, known as crowds. The progress to autonomy includes coordinating into these social designs, where more established kin, maternal figures, and other crowd individuals assume parts in the proceeded with development and learning of youthful kangaroos. We investigate the intricacies of horde elements and the agreeable ways of behaving that add to the outcome of kangaroo networks.

5. **Difficulties and Methods for surviving:**
Hunter Evasion Methods:
Endurance in the wild requires successful hunter evasion strategies. Youthful kangaroos foster methodologies, for example, jumping, boxing with strong rear legs, and looking for shelter in the security of the crowd. We dig into the complexities of these endurance strategies and their job in deeply shaping the way of behaving of kangaroos because of likely dangers.

Natural Variations:
The Australian scene presents a scope of natural difficulties, from outrageous temperatures to food shortage. Kangaroos exhibit versatility by creating physiological and social components to adapt to these difficulties. We investigate how kangaroos explore different biological systems, displaying their flexibility and capacity to flourish in shifted territories.

6. **Human-Natural life Collaboration:**
Urbanization and Living space Infringement:
As human exercises infringe on regular living spaces, kangaroos should adjust to a climate progressively formed by human presence. Urbanization, territory fracture, and experiences with human framework present difficulties for kangaroos. We analyze the elements of human-untamed life connection and the ramifications for the prosperity of kangaroo populaces.

Protection Difficulties and Drives:
Preservation endeavors for kangaroos face various difficulties, including environment misfortune, environmental change, and human-natural life clashes. We investigate the protection drives pointed toward safeguarding kangaroo environments, alleviating clashes, and carrying out feasible administration rehearses. The job of logical examination and local area commitment in protecting the eventual fate of kangaroo populaces is likewise analyzed.

7. **Social Importance and Imagery:**
Native Viewpoints:
Kangaroos hold social importance in Native Australian people group. Dreamtime stories, workmanship, and customary practices grandstand the profound association between Native individuals and kangaroos. We investigate the profound and emblematic components of kangaroos in Native societies, featuring the social lavishness implanted in the kangaroo's presence.

Public Imagery:
Past Native societies, kangaroos are meaningful of Australia on the worldwide stage. We dive into their job as a public image, including conspicuously on the nation's ensign and becoming inseparable from the exceptional natural life of the Australian mainland.

8. Logical Exploration and Innovative Headways:

Commitment to Near Science:

Kangaroos offer one of a kind experiences into near science, especially in regards to marsupial propagation, maternal consideration, and social elements. Logical examination on kangaroo nurturing adds to how we might interpret marsupial development and the more extensive setting of mammalian science.

Mechanical Apparatuses and Exploration Techniques:

Progressions in innovation play had a urgent impact in unwinding the mysteries of kangaroo nurturing. We investigate the utilization of GPS following, satellite symbolism, and hereditary examination as apparatuses that empower researchers to concentrate on kangaroos in their normal environments. The convergence of mechanical development and organic examination opens new roads for figuring out marsupial way of behaving.

B. Significance of Kangaroo Parenting in the Animal Kingdom

In the immense embroidery of the set of all animals, few nurturing techniques enrapture the creative mind very like that of kangaroos. Native to Australia, these marsupials have developed an unmistakable type of nurturing set apart by the notorious pocket, giving an extraordinary window into the complexities of nature's plan. This investigation digs into the meaning of kangaroo nurturing, unwinding the illustrations it offers concerning versatility, endurance, and the more extensive developmental scene inside the collective of animals.

1. Developmental Establishments: An Exceptional Way in Parental Consideration:

Marsupial Generation as a Transformative Specialty:

The developmental excursion of kangaroo nurturing starts with an investigation of marsupial proliferation. Diverging from placental vertebrates, marsupials show a special conceptive procedure where exceptionally lacking youthful are conceived and complete their initial improvement inside the defensive bounds of the pocket. This unmistakable way to deal with nurturing addresses a developmental specialty that has permitted marsupials to flourish in assorted biological systems.

Versatile Advantages of Marsupial Proliferation:

The meaning of kangaroo nurturing lies in the versatile advantages gave by marsupial proliferation. The birthing of immature youthful takes into consideration expanded versatility and adaptability, empowering marsupials to answer progressively to natural changes. We analyze how this versatile system has added to the achievement and variety of marsupials, exhibiting the creativity of nature's plan.

2. **Maternal Consideration as a Diagram for Versatility:**
   Pocket as a Microcosm of Supporting:
   The pocket fills in as a microcosm of maternal consideration, offering experiences into the versatility expected for effective nurturing. Inside this warm and defensive climate, joeys go through basic progressive phases, directed by maternal impulses and natural signs. We investigate the supporting parts of the pocket and its job in encouraging versatility in kangaroo posterity.
   Maternal Transformations and Adaptability:
   Kangaroo moms show a surprising degree of versatility in answering the requirements of their joeys. From changing milk structure to suit changing healthful prerequisites to giving a solid pocket climate during outside challenges, maternal versatility is a sign of kangaroo nurturing. This flexibility reaches out to conduct reactions, for example, changing prepping and defensive ways of behaving in light of natural signals.

3. **Methods for surviving and Social Variations:**
   Hunter Aversion: The Craft of Avoidance:
   Endurance in the wild requests compelling hunter evasion techniques. Kangaroos, with their strong rear legs and special movement style, have advanced a guileful way to deal with avoiding hunters. We dive into the meaning of these social variations, investigating how kangaroo nurturing furnishes joeys with the abilities expected to explore the difficulties of the Australian scene.
   Scrounging Transformations: Exploring Environmental Specialties:
   The meaning of kangaroo nurturing stretches out past the pocket to the scavenging ways of behaving conferred to youthful joeys. We investigate how joeys figure out how to recognize and adjust to different food sources, displaying the job of maternal direction in forming scrounging ways of behaving. These transformations feature the significance of environmental specialty specialization in the endurance and outcome of kangaroo populaces.

4. **Social Elements: Agreeable Living for Endurance:**
   Arrangement of Hordes and Helpful Nurturing:
   Kangaroos are social creatures that structure gatherings, or hordes, for common advantage. The meaning of these social designs lies in helpful nurturing, where moms as well as more established kin and other horde individuals add to the childhood of joeys. We disentangle the elements of kangaroo hordes, investigating how helpful living improves the endurance chances of individual joeys and the more extensive gathering.
   Correspondence inside Crowds: The Language of Endurance:
   Successful correspondence is fundamental for agreeable living inside kangaroo crowds. Vocalizations, non-verbal communication, and other specialized strategies act as a language of endurance, working with coordination during scavenging, hunter recognition, and collective exercises. The meaning of these

correspondence systems lies in their job as versatile components that upgrade the general flexibility of kangaroo networks.

5. **Human-Untamed life Connections: Exploring an Evolving Scene: Urbanization and Natural surroundings Discontinuity: Difficulties for Kangaroo Nurturing:**

Kangaroo nurturing faces remarkable difficulties in the Anthropocene, set apart by human-actuated changes to normal scenes. Urbanization, environment discontinuity, and experiences with human foundation present difficulties for kangaroos. We investigate the meaning of versatility even with these difficulties, taking into account the ramifications for the endurance and prosperity of kangaroo populaces.

Protection Suggestions: Adjusting Human Requirements and Kangaroo Endurance:

The protection meaning of kangaroo nurturing is personally attached to the sensitive harmony between human necessities and natural life safeguarding. We dive into preservation challenges, taking into account the effect of environment misfortune, environmental change, and human-untamed life clashes on kangaroo populaces.

The illustrations gained from kangaroo nurturing illuminate preservation procedures pointed toward cultivating concurrence and saving the versatile strength of these marsupials.

6. **Logical Experiences and Commitments:**

Marsupials as Transformative Contextual analyses:

Kangaroo nurturing fills in as a rich wellspring of logical request, giving important experiences into marsupial science and development. We investigate the meaning of kangaroos as developmental contextual analyses, revealing insight into the more extensive ramifications for how we might interpret mammalian multiplication, parental consideration, and versatile systems.

Mechanical Progressions in Kangaroo Exploration:

Mechanical devices and progressions play had a significant impact in opening the mysteries of kangaroo nurturing. From GPS following to satellite symbolism and hereditary examination, these apparatuses empower researchers to concentrate on kangaroos in their normal environments. The convergence of innovation and organic exploration improves our capacity to appreciate the intricacies of kangaroo conduct, adding to more extensive conversations in environment and protection.

7. **Social and Representative Importance: Kangaroos in Human Accounts:**

Native Points of view: Social Lavishness and Profound Association:

The social meaning of kangaroo nurturing is woven into the texture of Native Australian points of view. Dreamtime stories, craftsmanship, and customary practices feature the profound association between Native people group and kangaroos. We investigate the otherworldly and emblematic aspects, uncovering the social lavishness implanted in the kangaroo's presence in Native stories.

Public Imagery: Kangaroos as Symbols of Australia:

Kangaroos have risen above the domain of science to become public images of Australia. We dig into their importance in Australian character, from highlighting on the nation's ensign to becoming symbolic of the special natural life that characterizes the landmass. The persevering through portrayal of kangaroos highlights their notorious status in the aggregate creative mind of the country.

C. Analogies to Human Parenting

Nurturing, a general peculiarity, appears in different structures across the animals of the world collectively. While people might appear completely different from different species, the nurturing systems of different creatures frequently bear interesting relationships to our own. In this investigation, we draw matches between kangaroo nurturing and human nurturing, disentangling the common parts of supporting, variation, and relational peculiarities. Through these relationships, we gain special experiences into the general difficulties and delights intrinsic in the excursion of being a parent.

1. **Birth and Early Turn of events:**
   Marvel of Birth:
   In both human and kangaroo nurturing, the snapshot of pigmentations an extraordinary start. While human children rise up out of the belly, kangaroo joeys set out on an excursion from the birth channel to the pocket. The weakness and reliance of babies make a quick connection among parent and posterity, accentuating the all inclusive wonder enlivened by the marvel of birth.
   Pocket as an Image of Maternal Security:
   Comparable to the glow and security given by a human mother's hug, the kangaroo pocket fills in as an image of maternal insurance. The pocket turns into a safe house for joeys, offering a supporting climate where they get food, solace, and the closeness fundamental for early holding. This similarity features the instinctual drive of moms across species to give a place of refuge to their young.

2. **Maternal Consideration and Holding:**
   Supporting Through Touch and Vicinity:
   The significance of actual contact in cultivating maternal bonds is a common part of both human and kangaroo nurturing. Human moms support their babies, offering contact as a type of consolation and association. Additionally, kangaroo moms express friendship through prepping, licking, and consistent vicinity, supporting the meaning of material communications in building solid parent-kid connections.
   Natural Maternal Senses:

Human and kangaroo moms show natural maternal impulses, answering the requirements of their posterity with momentous responsiveness. Whether it's a human mother deciphering a child's cries or a kangaroo identifying unobtrusive signals from its joey, the natural comprehension among parent and kid rises above species limits. This common perspective stresses the significant close to home and instinctual aspects of nurturing.

3. **Early Learning and Investigation:**
Training Through Perception:
Practically equivalent to human babies noticing and copying their folks, kangaroo joeys master fundamental abilities through perception and impersonation inside the pocket. From the obtaining of coordinated abilities to understanding rummaging ways of behaving, the beginning phases of nurturing act as an instructive establishment. This equal highlights the general topic of learning through parental direction in the beginning phases of life.

Steady Change to Autonomy:
Both human and kangaroo guardians explore the fragile harmony between supporting reliance and empowering freedom. Human babies make their most memorable strides, investigating the world under the full concentrations eyes of their folks. Essentially, kangaroo joeys experience a progressive change from the pocket to freedom, displaying the normal subject of guardians working with the investigation and improvement of their young.

4. **Social Elements and Local area Backing:**
Helpful Nurturing in Hordes:
Kangaroos are social creatures that flourish in bunches known as crowds. The agreeable nurturing saw inside kangaroo crowds attracts equals to the human idea of local area support. More established kin, similar to human kin, assume parts in the childhood of more youthful joeys, representing the significance of common help with the nurturing venture.

Correspondence and Language Advancement:
Powerful correspondence is a foundation of nurturing in the two people and kangaroos. Human guardians take part in verbal correspondence, encouraging language advancement in their kids. Kangaroo guardians, however non-verbal, impart through vocalizations, non-verbal communication, and material prompts, underlining the general job of correspondence in supporting securities and guaranteeing the attachment of the nuclear family.

5. **Challenges and Versatile Reactions:**
Hunter Evasion Procedures:
Parental impulses for shielding posterity from potential dangers are all inclusive. Human guardians guarantee the wellbeing of their kids through carefulness and direction. Additionally, kangaroo guardians give step by step processes for surviving to joeys, showing them how to explore and stay away from hunters.

The common test of guaranteeing the security of posterity highlights the all inclusive nature of parental defensive impulses.

Ecological Variations:

Both human and kangaroo guardians face the test of adjusting to their particular surroundings. Human guardians give direction on exploring cultural standards and social assumptions, while kangaroo guardians confer abilities to survive custom fitted to the Australian outback. This equal features the normal topic of guardians setting up their posterity for the difficulties of the world they possess.

6. **Progress to Autonomy:**

Steady Arrival of Reliance:

The progress to freedom is a widespread achievement in nurturing. Human guardians witness their youngsters making their most memorable strides towards independence, reflecting the progressive arrival of reliance found in kangaroo nurturing. The common experience of working with this progress stresses the self-contradicting nature of watching posterity develop and acquire freedom.

Job of More distant family:

The two people and kangaroos frequently benefit from the help of more distant family structures. In human social orders, grandparents and more distant family individuals add to childcare and childhood. In kangaroo crowds, more established kin and different individuals assume parts in the aggregate nurturing exertion. This similarity highlights the meaning of expanded familial help in the more extensive setting of nurturing.

7. **Social and Profound Importance:**

Imagery in Native Societies:

The kangaroo, with its remarkable nurturing style, holds social importance in Native Australian people group. Undifferentiated from how creatures are loved in different human societies, kangaroos highlight conspicuously in Native stories, representing profound associations and tribal insight. This similarity features the common human propensity to attribute social and representative importance to specific creature species.

Public Images and Portrayals:

Similarly as kangaroos are notorious images of Australia, certain creatures hold emblematic significance in different human social orders. Public tokens, mascots, and social images frequently draw motivation from the animals of the world collectively. This similarity mirrors the common human tendency to celebrate and relate to specific creatures, hoisting them to symbolic status.

Chapter 1

The Pouch Chronicles

The perplexing universe of kangaroo nurturing unfurls inside the limits of the pocket, a special and fundamental part of marsupial life. This exposition investigates "The Pocket Annals," diving into the complexities of kangaroo nurturing, revealing insight into the physical, formative, and conduct aspects of this interesting peculiarity. As we leave on this investigation, we mean to disentangle the mysteries concealed inside the pocket and comprehend the meaning of kangaroo nurturing in the set of all animals.

Life systems of the Kangaroo Pocket

The kangaroo pocket, a pocket like overlap of skin, assumes a critical part in the conceptive procedure of marsupials. Not at all like placental warm blooded creatures, kangaroos bring forth somewhat lacking youthful, which then, at that point, proceed with their development and development inside the wellbeing of the pocket. The life systems of the pocket is a wonder of transformative variation, finely tuned to oblige the necessities of the creating posterity. This part investigates the actual qualities of the pocket, its developmental importance, and how it contrasts and pockets of different marsupials.

Formative Stages Inside the Pocket

When the little, untimely kangaroo is conceived, it leaves on a noteworthy excursion inside the pocket. This segment inspects the different formative stages experienced inside the pocket, zeroing in on the development and development of the posterity. Moreover, we dive into the dietary parts of pocket life, investigating the creation and utilization of milk as a fundamental part of the kangaroo's turn of events. Social changes inside the pocket, formed by the restricted space, are likewise investigated to give an extensive comprehension of this basic period in a kangaroo's life.

Kangaroo Nurturing Ways of behaving in Nature

The normal territory of kangaroos essentially impacts their nurturing ways of behaving. This part examines the manners by which kangaroos adjust their nurturing systems to natural variables, guaranteeing the endurance of their posterity. From the tremendous Australian wild to different environments, kangaroos show a scope of nurturing ways of behaving that mirror their flexibility and strength. Understanding these ways of behaving gives important experiences into the difficulties looked by kangaroo guardians in nature.

Maternal Consideration and Holding

One of the most charming parts of kangaroo nurturing is the maternal consideration given inside the pocket. This segment investigates the one of a kind components of maternal consideration, revealing insight into the supporting ways of behaving of kangaroo moms. The nearby bond framed during this period is vital for the endurance and advancement of the posterity. By looking at the complexities of maternal consideration, we gain a more profound appreciation for the intricate connection between kangaroo moms and their young, attracting equals to human parental senses and providing care ways of behaving.

Nourishing Procedures Inside the Pocket

The pocket isn't simply a defensive nook; it fills in as a supporting space where healthful systems become possibly the most important factor. This segment dives into the instruments of milk creation, its arrangement, and the way that it takes care of the particular requirements of creating kangaroo joeys. The dietary elements inside the pocket contribute fundamentally to the wellbeing and prosperity of the posterity, exhibiting the refinement of nature's plan in guaranteeing the endurance of marsupial species.

Helpful Nurturing and the Job of Kangaroo Fathers

While maternal consideration becomes the dominant focal point, kangaroo fathers assume a fundamental part in nurturing. This part investigates the agreeable nurturing elements, featuring the commitments of male kangaroos to the childhood of their young. From security to direction, kangaroo fathers display a scope of ways of behaving that supplement the maternal consideration gave inside the pocket. Understanding the novel commitments of the two guardians gives a comprehensive perspective on kangaroo nurturing and its transformative benefits.

Illustrations from Kangaroo Mothers and Fathers

As we disentangle the complexities of kangaroo nurturing, this segment draws significant illustrations that can be extrapolated to human nurturing. The intrinsic impulses, versatility, and flexibility showed by kangaroo guardians offer bits of knowledge that reverberate with the difficulties looked by current families. By looking at the procedures utilized in the wild, we gain a new viewpoint on successful nurturing methods, underlining the significance of collaboration, versatility, and sustaining connections among guardians and posterity.

Difficulties and Arrangements

Life in the pocket isn't without its difficulties. This part investigates the ecological dangers that kangaroo guardians face and the clever arrangements they utilize to guarantee the endurance of their posterity. From hunters to climatic changes, kangaroos display momentous strength and versatility, giving important illustrations to human guardians exploring the intricacies of the advanced world. Understanding the difficulties looked by kangaroo guardians reveals insight into the all inclusiveness of nurturing battles and the methodologies utilized to defeat them.

Logical Experiences: Exploration and Concentrates on Kangaroo Nurturing

Logical examination plays had a critical impact in disentangling the secrets of kangaroo nurturing. This part dives into the logical experiences collected from concentrates on kangaroo nurturing, looking at the procedures utilized and the commitments to how we might interpret parental way of behaving. From conduct perceptions to physiological examinations, established researchers has contributed fundamentally to the assemblage of information encompassing marsupial nurturing. The ramifications of these experiences for our more extensive comprehension of creature conduct and, likewise, human nurturing are investigated exhaustively.

Past the Pocket: Growing Up Kangaroo

Life outside the pocket denotes a huge change for kangaroo posterity. This segment looks at the slow shift from pocket to autonomy, investigating how youthful kangaroos adjust to their environmental factors, associate with peers, and incorporate into the kangaroo local area. Drawing matches with human youthfulness, we gain a more profound comprehension of the difficulties looked by youthful kangaroos as they explore the intricacies of the rest of the world. This segment underscores the significance of this temporary stage and its job in molding the eventual fate of kangaroo people inside the more extensive environment.

1.1 Anatomy of the Kangaroo Pouch

The kangaroo pocket remains as a surprising illustration of developmental variation, a particular design that assumes a critical part in the regenerative technique of marsupials. This paper leaves on a definite investigation of the life structures of the kangaroo pocket, diving into its actual qualities, developmental importance, and correlations with pockets of different marsupials. As we analyze the complexities of this one of a kind physical component, we plan to disentangle the secrets covered inside, revealing insight into how it works with the development and improvement of kangaroo posterity.

Actual Qualities of the Kangaroo Pocket

The kangaroo pocket is a particular physical element, a specific crease of skin situated on the ventral side of the marsupial's body. This segment investigates the actual qualities of the pocket, looking at its size, shape, and adaptability. Dissimilar to the externalized pockets of certain marsupials, the kangaroo pocket is inner, giving a safeguarded climate to the creating posterity. The game plan of muscles, tendons, and skin folds inside the pocket adds to its interesting design, guaranteeing a safe and sustaining space for the youthful kangaroo, known as a joey.

The pocket's size shifts among kangaroo species, reflecting variations to their particular environmental specialties. Bigger species might have more extensive pockets to oblige the developing joeys, while more modest species might have pockets custom-made to their specific necessities. The pocket's flexibility is a demonstration of the proficiency of nature's plan in fulfilling the needs of various kangaroo species.

Inside the pocket, specific mammary organs assume an essential part in sustaining the creating joey. The appropriation and construction of these mammary organs inside the pocket are fundamental parts of the kangaroo's conceptive system. Understanding the actual qualities of the pocket gives an establishment to disentangling its complicated capabilities in supporting the kangaroo's remarkable technique for proliferation.

Transformative Meaning of the Kangaroo Pocket

The development of the kangaroo pocket is a demonstration of the flexibility of marsupials to different conditions and regenerative difficulties. This segment digs into the transformative history of the pocket, inspecting the specific tensions and biological variables that leaned toward its turn of events. The pocket's rise addresses a critical development in marsupial regenerative methodologies, offering a particular benefit concerning posterity endurance.

The progress from inward to outside pockets in marsupials denotes a pivotal transformative achievement. The kangaroo pocket, being inward, gives upgraded security to the creating posterity, safeguarding them from outer dangers and natural circumstances. This part investigates how the development of the kangaroo pocket is unpredictably connected to the endurance and conceptive outcome of marsupials in different environments.

Correlations with other marsupial pockets shed light on the variety of regenerative procedures inside this scientific categorization. While kangaroos have an interior pocket, different marsupials, for example, wallabies and wombats, show externalized pockets. Understanding these varieties offers experiences into the versatile radiation of marsupials and the joined advancement of pocket structures in light of comparative conceptive difficulties.

Examinations with Pockets of Different Marsupials

While the kangaroo pocket is an unmistakable component, it imparts shared traits to pockets tracked down in different marsupials. This part investigates the similitudes and contrasts between the kangaroo pocket and pockets of species like wallabies, koalas, and wombats. Relative life systems gives significant bits of knowledge into the developmental directions that prompted the assorted exhibit of pocket structures saw in marsupials.

Wallabies, direct relations of kangaroos, have externalized pockets comparative in capability yet varying apparently. The underlying transformations of wallaby pockets reflect natural subtleties and the particular requirements of their young. Koalas, arboreal marsupials, have pockets adjusted for climbing and exploring the treetops. Wombats, burrowers conversely, have in reverse confronting pockets, keeping soil from entering as they dig.

Understanding these varieties adds to our more extensive comprehension of marsupial advancement and the complicated exchange among life structures and biological specialization. The examination of pocket structures across marsupials fills in as a rich embroidery, outlining the variety of conceptive procedures that have developed in light of various natural difficulties.

Useful Parts of the Kangaroo Pocket

The kangaroo pocket is in excess of a simple physical construction; it serves a huge number of capabilities fundamental for the endurance and prosperity of the creating posterity. This part analyzes the utilitarian parts of the pocket, investigating how it works with multiplication, parental consideration, and the progress from birth to freedom for kangaroo joeys.

Regenerative Help: The pocket gives a safeguarded climate to the lacking youthful, permitting them to proceed with their development and development outside the belly. The one of a kind conceptive system of kangaroos, named undeveloped diapause, empowers females to have various phases of posterity in various formative states all the while. The pocket goes about as a support for these creating joeys, guaranteeing their wellbeing and empowering the mother to concentrate on their consideration.

Parental Consideration: The kangaroo pocket is the focal point of parental consideration, especially maternal consideration. Female kangaroos put critical investment in focusing on their young inside the pocket. Mammary organs inside the pocket produce milk custom fitted to the particular necessities of the creating joeys, giving fundamental supplements to their development. The glow and security of the pocket establish an optimal climate for the weak posterity, encouraging a nearby connection among mother and joey.

Progress to Freedom: As joeys develop and foster inside the pocket, the pocket likewise fills in as a take off platform for their possible change to autonomy. The continuous openness to the outside climate permits joeys to adjust to their environmental factors while as yet profiting from the security of the pocket. This segment investigates the job of the pocket in planning joeys for the difficulties they will look outside, from creating coordinated abilities to adapting to ecological improvements.

Physiological Transformations Inside the Pocket

The physiological transformations inside the kangaroo pocket add to its multilayered capabilities. This segment dives into the complexities of mammary organ improvement, milk creation, and the remarkable qualities of kangaroo milk that take care of the particular necessities of creating joeys.

Mammary Organ Advancement: The plan and improvement of mammary organs inside the pocket are basic parts of the kangaroo's regenerative technique. The pocket houses a few sets of mammary organs, each related with a nipple. The quantity of nipples fluctuates among kangaroo species, impacting the regenerative limit of females. Understanding the physiological parts of mammary organ advancement gives bits of knowledge into the regenerative transformations that have developed in kangaroos.

Milk Creation: The pocket isn't simply a defensive space; it is a dietary center where milk creation supports the development and improvement of joeys. Kangaroo milk goes through a progression of compositional changes to meet the developing requirements of the developing posterity. This segment looks at the variables affecting milk creation, the organization of kangaroo milk, and how it contrasts and the milk of placental warm blooded creatures. The capacity of kangaroo moms to fit the sythesis of their milk to the particular necessities of their joeys exhibits the complexity of marsupial conceptive techniques.

Remarkable Qualities of Kangaroo Milk: Kangaroo milk is portrayed by its intricacy and flexibility. This part investigates the wholesome parts of kangaroo milk, including proteins, fats, and carbs. The presence of bioactive mixtures and antibodies in kangaroo milk adds to the resistant improvement of joeys, offering a degree of security not tracked down in placental well evolved creatures. The flexibility of kangaroo milk sythesis mirrors the unique exchange between maternal physiology and the advancing necessities of creating joeys inside the pocket.

1.2 Developmental Stages Inside the Pouch

The pocket, an exceptional and specific element of marsupials, fills in as a safe-haven for the improvement of their young. This exposition sets out on a top to bottom investigation of the formative stages inside the pocket, zeroing in on the development, development, and conduct changes of kangaroo posterity. As we dig into this multifaceted excursion inside the pocket, we plan to disentangle the secrets of how marsupials, especially kangaroos, explore the difficulties of early life and progress towards autonomy.

The Starting points: Birth and Section into the Pocket

The excursion inside the pocket starts with the introduction of a small, untimely kangaroo, known as a joey. Brought into the world in an early stage express, the joey is especially defenseless and lacking. This part examines the remarkable regenerative technique of kangaroos, named undeveloped diapause, which permits females to have various phases of posterity in various formative states at the same time.

Upon birth, the joey intuitively explores its direction to the mother's pocket, directed by a blend of olfactory and material signs. The most common way of entering the pocket is a sensitive and basic stage, where the mother's help is insignificant. This part investigates the difficulties looked by joeys during this underlying excursion, featuring the significance of their natural impulses and the job of maternal nearness.

Inside the pocket, the joey appends itself to one of the mother's nipples, starting the course of lactation. This denotes the start of a remarkable and close time of maternal consideration that assumes a key part in the resulting transformative phases.

Beginning phases of Advancement: The Neonatal Stage

The underlying weeks inside the pocket comprise the neonatal stage, a period portrayed by quick development and the foundation of indispensable physiological capabilities. This part analyzes the physiological variations of joeys during this stage, including the advancement of their stomach related and respiratory frameworks. The kangaroo pocket gives a controlled climate where temperature and moistness are directed, encouraging ideal circumstances for the weak child.

Mammary organs inside the pocket produce milk that is custom-made to the particular necessities of neonatal joeys. The sythesis of kangaroo milk goes through unique changes during this stage, giving fundamental supplements to the creating posterity. The neonatal stage is urgent for establishing the groundwork for resulting formative achievements, and the mother's interest in giving the ideal nourishing climate is central.

Maternal consideration during the neonatal stage stretches out past sustenance. This part investigates the social parts of maternal consideration, including the mother's prepping, insurance, and the foundation of a bond with her posterity.

The cozy contact among mother and joey inside the pocket cultivates profound associations that are imperative for the joey's prosperity and future turn of events.

Physiological and Social Variations: Mid-Pocket Improvement

As the joey advances through the neonatal stage, it goes through critical physiological and conduct variations. This part analyzes the advancement of tactile discernment, coordinated abilities, and the rise of additional mind boggling ways of behaving. Inside the pocket, the joey's eyes and ears open, permitting it to completely see the world external more. The improvement of these tactile capacities is fundamental for the joey's capacity to interface with its current circumstance.

Coordinated abilities likewise go through refinement during mid-pocket advancement. The restricted space inside the pocket requires the advancement of facilitated developments, laying the foundation for future headway. This part investigates the movement of coordinated abilities, from straightforward developments to additional mind boggling activities, as the joey adjusts to the imperatives of the pocket.

Social variations incorporate the investigation of the pocket climate and communications with the mother. The joey starts to display interest and fun loving nature, taking part in ways of behaving that add to its mental and actual turn of events. The mother's part in working with these exploratory ways of behaving is urgent, as she gives direction and consolation inside the bound space of the pocket.

Changing Towards Autonomy: Late-Pocket Advancement

The late-pocket improvement stage denotes a basic point as the joey gets ready for freedom outside the pocket. This part investigates the steady progress from complete dependence on the pocket to expanded independence. The advancement of social ways of behaving turns out to be more articulated as the joey connects with its mom and, if pertinent, different kin inside the pocket.

Physiologically, the joey's stomach related framework adjusts to oblige strong food in anticipation of weaning. This part looks at the dietary changes that happen during late-pocket improvement, including the presentation of plant material and the mother's job in working with the progress to a more different eating routine.

Coordinated movements proceed to refine, and the joey turns out to be progressively versatile inside the pocket. The mother's pocket gives a solid climate to the joey to rehearse fundamental locomotor abilities, making way for fruitful route in the outside climate. The joey's expanded versatility inside the pocket is demonstrative of its developing freedom and preparation for the following period of life.

Social Intricacy and Learning Inside the Pocket

Social intricacy inside the pocket stretches out past simple motion. This segment dives into the mental and social parts of joey advancement, including the securing of critical thinking abilities, correspondence with the mother, and connections with kin if present. The bound space of the pocket offers a controlled climate for the joey to improve these abilities, establishing the groundwork for fruitful combination into the rest of the world.

Perceptions of play conduct, prepping ceremonies, and social connections inside the pocket give experiences into the advancement of social bonds among kin, assuming various joeys share a similar pocket. The mother's job in working with these cooperations is significant for the foundation of progressive connections and social elements that add to the joey's general turn of events.

Advancing inside the pocket is a powerful interaction, impacted by both inborn elements and the outside climate. This segment investigates the manners by which joeys get information, adjust to evolving conditions, and acquire fundamental basic instincts. The mother's direction and the difficulties introduced inside the pocket add to the mental advancement of the joey, setting it up for the intricacies of life past the pocket.

Difficulties and Dangers Inside the Pocket Climate

While the pocket gives a protected and supporting climate for joeys, it isn't without difficulties and likely dangers. This segment inspects natural elements inside the pocket that might present dangers to the creating posterity. From microbial difficulties to the gamble of congestion, the pocket presents an extraordinary situation that joeys should explore for effective turn of events.

Microbial difficulties inside the pocket, including the potential for contaminations, feature the fragile harmony among assurance and openness. The invulnerable improvement of joeys inside the pocket is a urgent part of their capacity to endure possible dangers. Understanding the difficulties presented by microorganisms inside the pocket gives experiences into the coevolutionary elements among marsupials and their microbial surroundings.

The gamble of congestion inside the pocket, especially in species where various posterity might have similar pocket, presents difficulties connected with asset accessibility and rivalry. This part investigates the methodologies utilized by joeys to explore these difficulties, including progressive ways of behaving and variations that add to their general wellness.

1.3 How Kangaroo Parents Adapt to Pouch Parenting

Kangaroo nurturing, recognized by the utilization of a pocket for supporting and raising posterity, is a many-sided dance among science and climate. This article dives into the different manners by which kangaroo guardians adjust to pocket nurturing, incorporating physiological, social, and natural perspectives.

The development of these variations mirrors the intricacy of marsupial nurturing and reveals insight into the exceptional methodologies that have advanced north of millions of years.

Physiological Transformations for Pocket Nurturing

Kangaroo guardians have developed exceptional physiological variations to explore the difficulties presented by pocket nurturing. One key variation is the peculiarity of early stage diapause. Dissimilar to placental vertebrates, kangaroos can briefly end the advancement of an undeveloped organism, permitting them to all the while have various phases of posterity. This system guarantees that a joey can foster inside the pocket while another undeveloped organism stays in suspended liveliness, anticipating ideal natural circumstances for birth. The capacity to control the planning of birth is a basic variation that lines up with times of ideal assets and environment, improving the endurance possibilities of the posterity.

Another physiological transformation significant to pocket nurturing is the improvement of mammary organs inside the pocket. Kangaroo moms have different sets of mammary organs, each related with a nipple. This game plan permits them to sustain various joeys at the same time, tending to the test of really focusing on posterity at various transformative phases. The mammary organs go through powerful changes to meet the differing nourishing necessities of joeys inside the pocket, displaying the versatility of kangaroo guardians to give custom-made sustenance.

Moreover, the structure of kangaroo milk is a demonstration of their physiological transformations. Kangaroo milk is a complicated liquid that adjusts its creation to meet the changing dietary prerequisites of joeys. This variation is urgent for the different progressive phases inside the pocket, from the neonatal stage to late-pocket advancement. The milk contains proteins, fats, and starches, alongside bioactive mixtures that add to the invulnerable improvement of joeys. The capacity to give a particular and versatile milk piece highlights the refinement of kangaroo nurturing.

Social Variations in Pocket Nurturing

Kangaroo guardians display a scope of social transformations that add to effective pocket nurturing. One of the key social perspectives is the course of birth and passage into the pocket. Dissimilar to placental well evolved creatures, kangaroo joeys are brought into the world in a lacking state and should explore their direction to the pocket autonomously. This way of behaving, driven by intuition and directed by olfactory and material signs, is a basic variation that guarantees the joey's ideal section into the defensive climate of the pocket.

When inside the pocket, maternal consideration becomes the dominant focal point. Kangaroo moms take part in preparing, assurance, and holding ways of behaving that encourage the close to home and actual prosperity of their posterity.

This close contact inside the bound space of the pocket makes serious areas of strength for a between the mother and joey, giving fundamental solace and security. The conduct transformations of maternal consideration inside the pocket are significant for the endurance and advancement of the powerless joey.

As joeys progress through the formative stages inside the pocket, their ways of behaving develop. In the neonatal stage, joeys display instinctual ways of behaving connected with taking care of and keeping in touch with the mother's nipples. As they enter the mid-pocket and late-pocket advancement stages, investigation and play ways of behaving become more noticeable. These ways of behaving add to the mental and actual advancement of joeys, setting them up for the difficulties they will look outside the pocket.

Moreover, kangaroo guardians show versatile ways of behaving because of natural difficulties inside the pocket. The restricted space requires facilitated developments and changes in accordance with oblige developing joeys. Perceptions of joeys adjusting to the requirements of the pocket climate feature the conduct adaptability that is fundamental for effective pocket nurturing.

Natural Transformations in Pocket Nurturing

The actual pocket addresses an interesting ecological transformation for kangaroo guardians. It fills in as a safeguarded and directed space where ecological factors, for example, temperature and dampness are controlled. This controlled climate is especially urgent during the neonatal stage when joeys are generally helpless. The pocket gives a warm and get territory, guaranteeing ideal circumstances for the development and improvement of the creating posterity.

Be that as it may, the pocket climate isn't without its difficulties. Microbial dangers inside the pocket present possible dangers to creating joeys. Kangaroo guardians have advanced invulnerable methodologies to balance these dangers and safeguard their posterity. The versatile invulnerable arrangement of joeys is invigorated through openness to ecological microorganisms inside the pocket, adding to the improvement of a powerful resistant reaction.

Packing inside the pocket, particularly in species with different posterity, presents ecological difficulties connected with asset accessibility and contest. Kangaroo guardians and joeys display progressive ways of behaving to explore these difficulties. Perceptions of joeys inside the pocket adjusting to jammed conditions give experiences into the natural elements and asset allotment systems utilized by kangaroo guardians.

An Ensemble of Transformations in Kangaroo Pocket Nurturing

All in all, kangaroo guardians have coordinated an orchestra of variations that fit physiological, social, and ecological components to effectively explore pocket nurturing.

The physiological transformations, for example, early stage diapause, mammary organ advancement, and milk creation, feature the complexities of conceptive techniques custom-made to the novel difficulties of pocket nurturing.

Conduct transformations, from birth and section into the pocket to maternal consideration and the advancement of joey ways of behaving, highlight the unique exchange between instinctual ways of behaving and learned reactions inside the restricted space of the pocket. Ecological variations, including the controlled circumstances inside the pocket and safe reactions to microbial dangers, feature the harmony among assurance and openness to natural difficulties.

The tale of kangaroo pocket nurturing is a demonstration of the strength and versatility of marsupials notwithstanding various ecological tensions. It likewise offers a captivating look into the more extensive standards of transformative science, parental consideration, and the manners by which complex ways of behaving and physiological variations coevolve to guarantee the endurance and progress of posterity. The variations saw in kangaroo pocket nurturing contribute not exclusively to the prosperity of individual joeys yet in addition to the supportability of marsupial populaces in their separate environments.

Chapter 2

Kangaroo Parenting in the Wild

Kangaroo nurturing in the wild is a dazzling adventure of maternal consideration, conceptive procedures, and versatile ways of behaving that have developed more than large number of years. This paper sets out on a complete investigation of the complexities of kangaroo nurturing right at home. From the immense Australian scenes to the difficulties presented by hunters and ecological variables, kangaroo nurturing mirrors a sensitive harmony among endurance and the supporting of the future.

The Regular Environment: A Pot for Nurturing Systems

Kangaroos, famous marsupials local to Australia, have adjusted to a different scope of biological systems, from dry deserts to rich prairies. This segment dives into the impact of the normal environment on kangaroo nurturing methodologies. The tremendousness of the Australian wild presents the two open doors and difficulties, forming the manners by which kangaroos explore their jobs as guardians.

The open scenes of Australia furnish kangaroos with an exceptional benefit - perceivability. The capacity to distinguish hunters from a good ways impacts kangaroo nurturing ways of behaving, with a solid accentuation on carefulness and defensive measures. Kangaroo moms, specifically, show increased mindfulness, using their strong rear appendages for quick escapes when fundamental. The job of the climate in forming parental ways of behaving is clear in the essential choice of resting and brushing regions, as well as the foundation of social designs inside kangaroo networks.

Variations to Ecological Elements

Kangaroo nurturing is unpredictably woven into the texture of ecological transformations. This segment investigates how kangaroos have developed to flourish in different biological systems, each introducing its own arrangement of difficulties and valuable open doors. From the dry red deserts to the mild woods, kangaroo species feature a scope of variations that add to fruitful nurturing in nature.

One remarkable variation is the effective water protection components utilized by kangaroos in dry locales. This variation is especially basic for lactating moms, guaranteeing that they can give adequate hydration to their joeys even in water-scant conditions. Kangaroo nurturing, consequently, stretches out past direct providing care to incorporate variations that address the principal needs of the posterity.

Furthermore, kangaroos show social transformations to adapt to occasional changes and food accessibility. The rhythmic movement of assets impact regenerative cycles, affecting the planning of births and the passage of joeys into the pocket. Kangaroo nurturing is unpredictably connected to the recurrent examples of the climate, exhibiting a synchronization of regenerative techniques with natural elements.

Step by step processes for surviving: Kangaroo Nurturing Notwithstanding Hunters

The wild isn't without its dangers, and kangaroo nurturing includes a steady hit the dance floor with hunters. This segment digs into the systems utilized by kangaroo guardians to safeguard their weak posterity from likely dangers. The transformative weapons contest among hunters and prey has molded the ways of behaving and variations that characterize kangaroo nurturing within the sight of imposing enemies.

One of the key step by step processes for surviving is the utilization of speed and nimbleness. Kangaroo moms, with their strong rear appendages, can cover huge spans in quick runs, giving a method for get out from hunters. This segment analyzes the multifaceted movement of shifty moves and the transmission of such abilities to creating joeys. The job of ecological elements, for example, the territory and vegetation, in molding get away from methodologies is likewise investigated.

One more pivotal part of endurance is the actual pocket. The pocket serves as a sustaining space as well as a defensive nook. Joeys can withdraw into the security of the pocket when confronted with approaching risk. Perceptions of kangaroo nurturing ways of behaving uncover occurrences where moms decisively utilize the pocket as a safeguard, putting themselves among hunters and their young.

Maternal Consideration: The Heartbeat of Kangaroo Nurturing

At the center of kangaroo nurturing is maternal consideration, a mind boggling exchange of ways of behaving and physiological variations that guarantee the prosperity and endurance of posterity. This segment analyzes the diverse components of maternal consideration, from birth and section into the pocket to the weaning of joeys. The intrinsic impulses and learned ways of behaving of kangaroo moms are fundamental to the progress of their nurturing tries.

The course of birth and section into the pocket is a basic crossroads in kangaroo nurturing. Not at all like placental well evolved creatures, kangaroo joeys are brought into the world in a profoundly lacking state and should explore their direction into the pocket freely. This segment investigates the mechanics of birth, the job of maternal direction during the section into the pocket, and the meaning of this underlying stage in laying out the connection among mother and joey.

When inside the pocket, maternal consideration takes different structures. Preparing ways of behaving are not only for neatness but rather additionally reinforce the connection among mother and joey. Kangaroo moms show a surprising aversion to the requirements of their posterity, changing their providing care ways of behaving to the formative phase of the joey. The restricted space of the pocket gives a cozy climate to these collaborations, cultivating profound associations essential for the joey's prosperity.

The job of mammary organs inside the pocket is vital to maternal consideration. The physiological transformations of kangaroo moms incorporate the capacity to create milk with a sythesis that develops to meet the changing nourishing necessities of joeys. This segment investigates the dietary parts of maternal consideration, analyzing the constituents of kangaroo milk and how it adds to the development and advancement of joeys inside the pocket.

Helpful Nurturing: The Job of Kangaroo Fathers

While maternal consideration is a point of convergence, kangaroo nurturing likewise includes helpful endeavors, especially from male kangaroos. This part investigates the job of kangaroo fathers in supporting nurturing tries. While not straightforwardly associated with pocket nurturing, male kangaroos add to the endurance and security of their posterity in unmistakable ways.

Male kangaroos, or boomers, assume a critical part in keeping a defensive border around females with joeys. Their watchfulness and strength act as a hindrance to expected hunters, establishing a more secure climate for moms and joeys to brush and rest. The agreeable idea of kangaroo nurturing stretches out past individual families to envelop social designs inside kangaroo networks, where the aggregate endeavors of guys add to the general wellbeing of the gathering.

Formative Stages and Learning in Nature

Kangaroo nurturing in the wild unfurls across different formative stages, each introducing novel difficulties and open doors. This part investigates how the wild fills in as a powerful homeroom for joeys, offering open doors for mastering fundamental abilities to survive. From the investigation of the climate inside the pocket to the progressive change to freedom, kangaroo nurturing includes a continuum of growth opportunities for the youthful.

The bound space of the pocket fills in as a defensive case during the neonatal stage. Joeys, in their lacking state, participate in instinctual ways of behaving connected with taking care of and keeping in touch with the mother's nipples. As they progress through mid-pocket and late-pocket improvement, ways of behaving shift towards investigation and play. The pocket climate turns into a space for the improvement of coordinated movements, tactile discernment, and social cooperations.

Learning in the wild stretches out past the pocket, with joeys bit by bit adjusting to the outside climate. Perceptions of play conduct, associations with kin, and reactions to natural improvements give bits of knowledge into the mental advancement of joeys. The wild turns into a material for leveling up fundamental endurance abilities, from rummaging for food to sidestepping hunters. Kangaroo nurturing, in this manner, includes not just the arrangement of care inside the pocket yet in addition the assistance of opportunities for growth that plan joeys for the difficulties of autonomous living.

Difficulties and Dangers to Kangaroo Nurturing in Nature

The wild, regardless of its tremendousness and overflow, presents difficulties and dangers to kangaroo nurturing. This part analyzes the ecological elements and anthropogenic impacts that influence the outcome of kangaroo nurturing right at home.

Dry spells, a common peculiarity in Australia, present critical difficulties to kangaroo nurturing. The shortage of water and decreased food assets impact regenerative cycles and the endurance possibilities of joeys. Kangaroo moms should explore these times of natural pressure, adjusting their nurturing procedures to guarantee the prosperity of their posterity.

Anthropogenic elements, including territory misfortune and fracture, acquaint extra difficulties with kangaroo nurturing. Urbanization and horticultural extension infringe upon customary kangaroo environments, prompting expanded human-natural life clashes. Street traffic represents an immediate danger to kangaroo guardians and joeys, bringing about wounds and fatalities. This segment investigates the effect of human exercises on kangaroo nurturing and the protection endeavors pointed toward alleviating these difficulties.

Protection Suggestions and Future Points of view

The difficulties looked by kangaroo nurturing in the wild have more extensive ramifications for the protection of these notable marsupials. This part analyzes the preservation status of kangaroo species, the job of safeguarded regions in protecting their regular living spaces, and the continuous exploration endeavors pointed toward understanding and relieving dangers to kangaroo nurturing.

Protection drives center around keeping up with the biological respectability of kangaroo territories and tending to the difficulties presented by environmental change, territory misfortune, and human-untamed life clashes. The job of public mindfulness and local area commitment in encouraging concurrence among people and kangaroos is likewise featured. By understanding the complexities of kangaroo nurturing in the wild, preservationists can foster designated techniques to guarantee the proceeded with endurance and prosperity of these exceptional marsupials.

2.1 Natural Habitat and Environmental Factors

The regular living space is the foundation of biodiversity, giving a different cluster of biological systems that help the complicated trap of life on The planet. This exposition leaves on a thorough investigation of regular natural surroundings and the urgent job of ecological variables in forming these biological systems. From the rich rainforests to the parched deserts, the normal territory is a powerful material where the exchange of environment, geology, and organic cooperations makes the circumstances for life to prosper.

The Variety of Normal Living spaces

Normal territories length a tremendous range, incorporating earthly, oceanic, and marine conditions. This part dives into the extravagance of earthly natural surroundings, including woodlands, meadows, deserts, and tundras, each described by special climatic circumstances and vegetation. The primary intricacy of woods, for example, gives a bunch of specialties to different greenery, while the sweeping prairies support notable herbivores and their hunters.

Oceanic natural surroundings, going from freshwater lakes to estuaries and wetlands, exhibit an alternate element of biodiversity. The flexibility of sea-going life forms to fluctuated water conditions features the powerful idea of these living spaces. Essentially, marine natural surroundings, from coral reefs to the untamed sea, harbor a stunning variety of marine life, stressing the interconnectedness of biological systems across the globe.

Environment as a Deciding Element

Environment remains as one of the essential determinants molding normal living spaces. This part investigates how temperature, precipitation, and occasional varieties impact the qualities of various living spaces. Tropical rainforests, described by high temperatures and bountiful precipitation, cultivate the development of different plant species and backing an abundance of creature life. Conversely, deserts, with their outrageous temperatures and negligible precipitation, are home to extraordinarily adjusted widely varied vegetation equipped for enduring bone-dry circumstances.

The mild zones, set apart by unmistakable seasons, make natural surroundings where species should explore changes in temperature and asset accessibility. This inconstancy cultivates transformations like hibernation, movement, and occasional rearing ways of behaving. Polar districts, with their cold temperatures, are occupied by species furnished with specific transformations, epitomizing the flexibility of life in outrageous conditions.

Geology and Topographical Elements

The actual highlights of the scene, including geology and topography, assume a crucial part in molding normal living spaces. This segment investigates how mountains, valleys, fields, and waterways add to the variety of living spaces. Mountains, with their elevational angles, make zones of shifting temperatures and vegetation, known as altitudinal zones. Valleys and fields, then again, may highlight particular soil types and water accessibility, affecting the kinds of plants and creatures that can flourish here.

Waterways, from streams and lakes to seas, comprise interesting environments that help sea-going life. Stream biological systems, for instance, display an inclination of stream speeds, impacting the kinds of living beings that can occupy various segments. Coral reefs, tracked down in tropical marine conditions, are biodiversity areas of interest where the actual construction of coral settlements gives safe house and food to a huge number of marine species.

Soil Arrangement and Supplement Cycling

Underneath the surface, soil creation assumes a significant part in deciding the sorts of plants that can flourish in a given living space. This part dives into the elements affecting soil richness, including the presence of natural matter, mineral substance, and microbial networks. Rich, fruitful soils support thick vegetation, making living spaces with high biodiversity.

The course of supplement cycling, where natural matter is decayed and gotten back to the dirt, is essential to the wellbeing of normal living spaces. Decomposers, for example, microscopic organisms and growths, separate dead plant and creature matter, delivering supplements that feed plants. This repeating system guarantees the maintainability of environments and features the interconnectedness of the living life forms inside a territory.

Organic Communications: Cornerstone Species and Biodiversity

Organic communications, including predation, rivalry, and mutualism, shape the elements of regular territories. This segment investigates the idea of cornerstone species, whose presence lopsidedly affects the construction and capability of an environment. Instances of cornerstone species, for example, hunters that control herbivore populaces or pollinators that work with plant propagation, delineate the flowing impacts their presence or nonappearance can have on biodiversity.

The many-sided trap of trophic collaborations, from makers to buyers and decomposers, supports the progression of energy inside environments. Biodiversity, the assortment of life inside a territory, is impacted by these communications. Elevated degrees of biodiversity add to the flexibility and steadiness of biological systems, improving their capacity to endure aggravations and adjust to evolving conditions.

Transformations to Natural Variables

Normal determination, the main thrust of development, has prompted a bunch of transformations that empower species to flourish in unambiguous ecological circumstances. This part looks at how life forms have advanced physiological, social, and morphological variations to adapt to natural difficulties. From the disguised tinge of prey species to the intensity resilience of desert-staying plants, transformations are custom-made to the exceptional requests of every natural surroundings.

Physiological variations, for example, the capacity of specific creatures to endure outrageous temperatures or use particular metabolic pathways, permit species to take advantage of explicit specialties inside a living space. Conduct transformations, including movement, hibernation, and mating customs, reflect procedures for endurance and generation. Morphological variations, for example, the state of bills in birds or the construction of plant leaves, are actual elements that improve a living being's wellness in its current circumstance.

Progression and Environmental Elements

Normal natural surroundings are not static; they go through changes over the long haul through an interaction known as environmental progression. This part investigates the idea of essential and auxiliary progression, where new natural surroundings foster over already desolate or upset regions. Trailblazer species, with their capacity to colonize brutal conditions, prepare for additional complicated environments to lay out.

The peak local area, a steady and mature environment, addresses the endpoint of progression. The arrangement of species and the design of the environment go through changes during progression, affected by elements like soil improvement, rivalry, and aggravations. Understanding the elements of environmental progression gives experiences into the versatility of biological systems and their ability for recovery.

Human Effect on Normal Living spaces

Human exercises, from deforestation to contamination, apply significant effects on normal territories. This part analyzes the manners by which anthropogenic variables add to living space corruption and loss of biodiversity. Deforestation, driven by farming development and logging, brings about the deficiency of critical natural surroundings for incalculable species and upsets environments on a worldwide scale.

Urbanization adjusts the scene, dividing environments and making boundaries to untamed life development. The change of regular natural surroundings into metropolitan regions adds to living space misfortune and stances challenges for species that can't adjust to human-ruled conditions. Contamination, including air and water contamination, presents poisons that can hurt living beings inside environments, prompting decreases in biodiversity.

Environmental change, driven by human-instigated factors like ozone harming substance emanations, represents a critical danger to regular territories. Climbing temperatures, modified precipitation examples, and outrageous climate occasions can upset natural adjusts and challenge the flexibility of species. This part investigates the flowing impacts of environmental change on natural surroundings and the criticalness of worldwide endeavors to alleviate its effect.

Preservation and Rebuilding Endeavors

Perceiving the significance of saving normal living spaces, preservation endeavors expect to alleviate the effects of human exercises and shield biodiversity. This part investigates preservation methodologies, including safeguarded regions, environment rebuilding, and practical asset the board. Safeguarded regions, for example, public parks and untamed life saves, act as shelters for biodiversity by giving undisturbed territories and working with natural cycles.

Natural surroundings reclamation includes endeavors to restore corrupted environments, once again introduce local species, and improve living space network. Reclamation projects add to the recuperation of biological systems influenced by human exercises, offering a brief look into the versatility of nature whenever offered the chance to bounce back. Supportable asset the executives centers around offsetting human necessities with the preservation of environments, guaranteeing the mindful utilization of regular assets.

Training and Mindfulness for Environment Preservation

Training and mindfulness assume significant parts in encouraging a more profound comprehension of the worth of regular environments and the requirement for preservation. This part investigates the significance of natural schooling in sustaining a feeling of obligation and stewardship towards the climate. Mindfulness crusades, resident science drives, and local area commitment endeavors add to building an aggregate obligation to territory preservation.

By ingraining an appreciation for biodiversity and environments, instruction engages people to settle on informed decisions that line up with preservation objectives. Understanding the interconnectedness of natural surroundings and the sensitive equilibrium of biological cycles upgrades the limit of networks to take part in environment preservation endeavors effectively.

2.2 Survival Instincts and Adaptations

Endurance impulses and transformations are the foundations of life's capacity to persevere and flourish in different conditions. This article investigates the multifaceted exchange between endurance senses and developmental variations, diving into the components that empower species to explore the difficulties of presence.

From the crucial drive to make due to the noteworthy variations that have developed north of millions of years, the tale of endurance is a demonstration of the strength and resourcefulness of life on The planet.

The Early stage Desire to Get by

At the core of each and every living creature lies a base inclination to get by. This part digs into the principal parts of endurance impulses, looking at the hereditary and conduct characteristics that are designed into the texture of life. The drive to endure is a general power that rises above species, appearing in ways of behaving like looking for food, staying away from hunters, and recreating to guarantee the congruity of life.

The hereditary underpinning of endurance senses is implanted in the DNA of each and every creature. Impulses are inheritable qualities that have developed through normal choice, inclining toward people with versatile ways of behaving that increment their possibilities of endurance. From the instinctual reactions of microorganisms to natural upgrades to the mind boggling ways of behaving of warm blooded creatures, endurance senses are a dynamic and developing part of life.

Transformation as Nature's Reaction to Difficulties

Transformation is nature's reaction to the consistently changing difficulties presented by the climate. This part investigates the idea of variation as a unique interaction that unfurls over ages, forming the qualities and attributes of species. The capacity to adjust is a sign of developmental achievement, permitting creatures to take advantage of new natural specialties, beat dangers, and flourish in different environments.

Developmental transformations happen at numerous levels, from the sub-atomic changes inside cells to the mind boggling ways of behaving displayed by life forms. This segment inspects instances of transformations across different taxa, featuring the variety of procedures that have advanced. From the disguise of chameleons to the anti-toxin opposition of microbes, variations are finely tuned reactions to specific tensions that shape the direction of development.

Physiological Transformations for Natural Difficulties

Endurance in different conditions requires physiological variations that empower creatures to adapt to explicit difficulties. This part investigates how living beings have advanced physiological instruments to control temperature, get and deal with supplements, and explore the complexities of their natural surroundings. Instances of physiological variations range from the thermoregulation of reptiles to the osmo-regulation of marine living beings.

In bone-dry conditions, where water is scant, organic entities have created components to limit water misfortune. Desert-adjusted plants might have specific leaves to diminish happening, while creatures might show concentrated pee to monitor water.

On the other hand, in oceanic conditions, organic entities face the test of keeping up with osmotic equilibrium. Variations, for example, particular gills in fish and salt-discharging organs in marine birds mirror the variety of physiological procedures that have advanced.

Social Transformations for Endurance

Social transformations are fundamental to a creature's endurance tool stash, empowering it to answer progressively to natural signals and difficulties. This part investigates a range of conduct transformations, from hunter evasion techniques to complex mating ceremonies. The capacity to change conduct because of ecological upgrades is a critical figure the outcome of numerous species.

Hunter prey communications epitomize the many-sided dance of social variations. Prey species might display obscure tinge, mimicry, or guarded ways of behaving to avoid hunters. On the other hand, hunters utilize hunting methodologies, correspondence strategies, and helpful ways of behaving to get their prey. The weapons contest among hunter and prey ways of behaving is a demonstration of the continuous development of methods for surviving.

Transitory ways of behaving address one more intriguing element of transformation. Species going from birds to whales attempt epic excursions to take advantage of occasional assets or break negative circumstances. The accuracy of transient courses and the capacity to explore immense distances address the complexity of conduct transformations sharpened over ages.

Primary and Morphological Transformations

The actual structure and construction of organic entities, formed by a long period of time of development, frequently uncover momentous variations to their surroundings. This segment investigates underlying and morphological variations, going from the specific limbs of arthropods to the smoothed out assortments of amphibian creatures. These variations are finely tuned to upgrade a creature's capacity to take care of, move, and get by in its natural specialty.

The variety of mouth shapes in birds is an exemplary illustration of morphological transformation connected with taking care of propensities. Finches with various bill shapes on the Galápagos Islands delineate how varieties in structure are chosen in light of the accessibility of explicit food sources. Essentially, the appendages of warm blooded creatures adjusted to various methods of velocity, like the wings of bats or the flippers of seals, feature the flexibility of morphological variations.

Underlying variations stretch out to the tiny level, where organic entities might have specific elements for endurance. Models incorporate the surface designs of microorganisms that empower them to stick to have tissues, or the minuscule designs of plant leaves that upgrade photosynthesis. These variations at the cell and sub-atomic levels add to the general progress of species in their surroundings.

Conceptive Methodologies: Guaranteeing the Coherence of Life

Conceptive methodologies are crucial transformations that guarantee the progression of life. This segment investigates how living beings have developed assorted conceptive procedures, from productive proliferation to fastidious parental consideration. The harmony among amount and nature of posterity mirrors the particular tensions and biological specialties that shape regenerative variations.

R-tacticians, portrayed by high conceptive rates, produce countless posterity with insignificant parental venture. Conversely, K-tacticians display lower regenerative rates yet put additional time and assets being taken care of by their couple of posterity. Instances of conceptive variations range from the productive egg-laying of bugs to the supporting ways of behaving of mammalian guardians.

Perplexing romance ceremonies and mating shows address social variations related with propagation. These ways of behaving, frequently molded by sexual choice, add to the fruitful matching of mates and the transmission of good characteristics to the future. The variety of regenerative procedures across the set of all animals features the flexibility of life to assorted environmental settings.

Helpful and Social Variations

Helpful and social ways of behaving have developed in numerous species, adding to the endurance and progress of people inside a gathering. This segment investigates how social variations, from agreeable hunting to complex correspondence frameworks, upgrade the wellness of people and the attachment of gatherings. Social designs, like provinces, groups, and packs, epitomize the advantages of cooperative living.

In friendly bugs like insects and honey bees, agreeable ways of behaving are fundamental for undertakings, for example, searching, home structure, and protection. Correspondence through pheromones or mind boggling moves works with coordination inside the state. Social well evolved creatures, for example, wolves and elephants, show complex ordered progressions and helpful hunting techniques that upgrade their capacity to get assets and safeguard their young.

Philanthropic ways of behaving, where people might forfeit individual readiness to serve the gathering, address a captivating component of social variations. Models incorporate alert brings in meerkats or helpful nurturing in specific bird species. These ways of behaving challenge conventional thoughts of individual-driven normal choice and highlight the significance of collective vibes in the endurance of species.

Human Endurance Impulses and Social Transformations

While the development of endurance impulses and transformations has formed the regular world, people, as well, have a rich embroidery of variations that have permitted our species to flourish across different conditions. This part looks at human endurance impulses, from the instinctive reaction to the supporting ways of behaving related with providing care.

Social variations address an extraordinary component of human endurance. The improvement of devices, language, and social designs has empowered people to over-come new conditions and team up on a scale unrivaled in the set of all animals. This segment investigates the job of culture in forming versatile ways of behaving, from the improvement of agribusiness to the foundation of perplexing social orders.

The mental capacities of people, including critical thinking, development, and the transmission of information across ages, play had a significant impact in our pros-perity as an animal groups. Social variations, communicated through advancements, customs, and conviction frameworks, have permitted people to explore a huge range of conditions and difficulties, exhibiting the powerful transaction among science and culture in the narrative of human endurance.

Difficulties to Endurance in the Cutting edge World

While endurance impulses and transformations have served species well over developmental timescales, the fast changes achieved by human exercises present new difficulties. This part investigates the effect of natural surroundings annihilation, con-tamination, environmental change, and other anthropogenic elements on the endur-ance of species around the world. The capacity of species to adjust to these uncommon difficulties will shape the direction of biodiversity in the next few decades.

Protection endeavors and methodologies for alleviating the effect of human exer-cises on normal living spaces are fundamental for shielding the endurance of innumer-able species. This part looks at the job of protection science, natural surroundings reclamation, and manageable practices in addressing the dangers to biodiversity. The criticalness of worldwide coordinated effort in safeguarding biological systems and protecting the versatile capability of species highlights the obligation of humankind in molding the eventual fate of life on The planet.

2.3 Observations of Kangaroo Parenting Behaviors

Kangaroo nurturing ways of behaving offer a spellbinding look into the complex-ities of maternal consideration and methods for surviving utilized by these notorious marsupials. Through sharp perceptions of kangaroo moms and their joeys, specialists and natural life lovers the same have uncovered a rich embroidery of ways of behav-ing that highlight the versatility and flexibility of kangaroo nurturing in different conditions.

Birth and Passage into the Pocket

One of the most captivating parts of kangaroo nurturing is the course of birth and the section of joeys into the pocket. Not at all like placental well evolved creatures, kangaroos bring forth profoundly lacking youthful, no bigger than a lima bean. Perceptions uncover that kangaroo moms display exceptional awareness during this basic stage. The mother helps the joey in its excursion from the birth waterway to the pocket, utilizing her forelimbs to direct the small, wriggling animal. This underlying holding second lays out the establishment for the extraordinary connection among mother and joey.

When inside the pocket, joeys keep on depending on their mom for sustenance and insurance. Kangaroo moms have been noticed changing the pocket opening to work with nursing and guaranteeing the joey's safe connection to a nipple. The restricted space of the pocket gives a personal climate where maternal consideration starts decisively.

Maternal Consideration Inside the Pocket

The pocket turns into a safe-haven of warmth and security, where kangaroo moms participate in a horde of supporting ways of behaving. Preparing, an apparently straightforward demonstration, takes on significant importance. Kangaroo moms utilize their tongues to tenderly spotless and groom their joeys, cultivating a bond that goes past simple cleanliness. This prepping conduct is accepted to reinforce the profound association among mother and joey, laying the preparation for trust and reliance.

The maternal pocket likewise fills in as a space for the complicated dance of nursing and milk utilization. Perceptions uncover that kangaroo moms have mammary organs fit for delivering milk customized to the changing dietary necessities of joeys at various progressive phases. The demonstration of nursing isn't just a wellspring of sustenance yet in addition a method for correspondence, as kangaroo moms change their stance and answer the signals of their joeys.

Kangaroo Mothers as Defenders

The wild is laden with difficulties, and kangaroo moms show a sharp feeling of carefulness and defensive impulses. Perceptions of kangaroo nurturing ways of behaving frequently feature the mother's job as a defender, utilizing her strong rear appendages to stand watch and utilizing quick moves to sidestep expected dangers. The actual pocket turns into a shelter, where joeys can withdraw notwithstanding risk, stressing the essential meaning of this novel marsupial transformation.

Kangaroo moms have been noticed involving the pocket as a safeguard, setting themselves between likely hunters and their weak youthful. The blend of speed, nimbleness, and maternal senses makes a considerable line of protection against the dangers of the Australian wild.

This defensive way of behaving isn't just a demonstration of the methods for surviving sharpened throughout developmental time yet in addition an outline of the profound connection among mother and joey.

Learning and Improvement Inside the Pocket

The bound space of the pocket fills in as an instructive field for joeys, where they go through a progression of formative stages. Perceptions uncover that the neonatal stage is described by instinctual ways of behaving connected with taking care of and keeping in touch with the mother's nipples. As joeys progress through mid-pocket and late-pocket advancement, ways of behaving shift towards investigation and play.

The pocket climate turns into a material for the improvement of coordinated movements, tactile insight, and social connections. Kangaroo joeys have been noticed participating in fun loving ways of behaving, including delicate wrestling and bouncing developments inside the pocket. These exercises add to the advancement of coordination and interactive abilities, planning joeys for the difficulties they will look after arising out of the pocket.

Autonomy and Then some

Perceptions reach out past the limits of the pocket to catch the progress to freedom. As joeys grow out of the pocket, they keep on depending on their moms for direction and security. Kangaroo nurturing ways of behaving incorporate the progressive acquaintance of joeys with the outside climate, where they figure out how to scavenge for food and explore the intricacies of nature.

The job of kangaroo fathers, or boomers, additionally becomes evident as joeys adventure into the world. Male kangaroos add to the security of the gathering, keeping a defensive edge around females and joeys. The agreeable idea of kangaroo nurturing reaches out past the mother-posterity dyad to envelop the more extensive social elements inside kangaroo networks.

Natural Difficulties and Variations

Perceptions of kangaroo nurturing ways of behaving additionally shed light on how these marsupials adjust to natural difficulties. Dry season, a repetitive peculiarity in Australia, presents huge obstacles for kangaroo nurturing. Kangaroo moms, outfitted with an intense consciousness of their environmental elements, should explore times of diminished water and food accessibility. Conduct transformations, for example, changes in brushing designs and vital determination of resting regions, are seen as kangaroos fight with the rhythmic movement of assets in their territories.

Human-natural life clashes, frequently filled by territory misfortune and urbanization, present extra difficulties for kangaroo nurturing. Perceptions in regions where human advancement infringes on customary kangaroo territories uncover the flexibility of these marsupials in adjusting to evolving scenes. Understanding the elements of kangaroo nurturing despite ecological difficulties is vital for informed preservation endeavors.

Chapter 3

Lessons from Kangaroo Moms

In the immense and various scenes of Australia, kangaroo moms stand as meaningful figures of strength, supporting, and flexibility. Their novel nurturing ways of behaving, molded by a long period of time of development, offer significant experiences into the intricacies of life. This investigation digs into the universe of kangaroo parenthood, disentangling the examples implanted in their maternal systems, the difficulties they explore, and the striking flexibility that characterizes their reality.

Grasping Kangaroo Parenthood

Kangaroo parenthood is particularly marsupial, portrayed by the pocket and the extraordinary formative direction of joeys. Dissimilar to placental well evolved creatures, kangaroos bring forth profoundly lacking youthful, no bigger than a lima bean. The course of birth and the resulting passage of joeys into the pocket mark the beginning of the complex excursion of kangaroo parenthood.

Birth and Passage into the Pocket: A Fragile Dance

The birthing system among kangaroos is a demonstration of the sensitive idea of life in nature. Kangaroo moms help their joeys as they venture from the birth channel to the pocket, utilizing their forelimbs to direct the minuscule, wriggling animals. This underlying holding second makes way for the close connection among mother and joey.

When inside the pocket, joeys proceed with their turn of events, depending on their mom for sustenance and insurance. The pocket turns into a safe-haven of warmth and security, encouraging an association that goes past the physical. Seeing this cycle offers a brief look into the delicacy and care intrinsic in kangaroo parenthood.

Maternal Consideration Inside the Pocket: Preparing, Nursing, and Holding

The pocket fills in as a private space where maternal consideration unfurls. Kangaroo moms take part in preparing ways of behaving, utilizing their tongues to clean and sustain their joeys. This apparently straightforward demonstration goes past cleanliness, laying out a connection among mother and joey that is primary to their relationship.

Nursing inside the pocket is a dynamic and significant part of kangaroo parenthood. The mother changes the pocket opening to work with nursing, guaranteeing the joey's solid connection to a nipple. The restricted space of the pocket turns into a domain of sustenance and solace, where the mother's consideration is complicatedly woven into the texture of the joeys' initial turn of events.

Kangaroo Mothers as Defenders: Cautiousness and Guarded Systems

The wild is a domain laden with difficulties, and kangaroo moms show a sharp feeling of carefulness and defensive impulses. Perceptions uncover their job as defenders, utilizing strong rear appendages to stand monitor and utilizing quick moves to avoid possible dangers. The pocket becomes a supporting space as well as a shelter where joeys can withdraw despite risk.

Kangaroo moms have been noticed involving the pocket as a safeguard, setting themselves between expected hunters and their weak youthful. This defensive way of behaving isn't just a demonstration of the step by step processes for surviving sharpened throughout developmental time yet additionally a representation of the profound connection among mother and joey. Kangaroo parenthood is an amicable mix of sustaining and watchful insurance.

Learning and Advancement Inside the Pocket: Energetic Investigation

The bound space of the pocket fills in as an instructive field for joeys. Perceptions uncover the progressive phases inside the pocket, from instinctual ways of behaving connected with taking care of to fun loving investigation as joeys develop. The pocket climate turns into a material for the improvement of coordinated movements, tangible discernment, and social cooperations.

Kangaroo joeys take part in fun loving ways of behaving, including delicate wrestling and jumping developments inside the pocket. These exercises add to the advancement of coordination and interactive abilities, getting ready joeys for the difficulties they will look after arising out of the pocket. Kangaroo parenthood, in this specific situation, encourages a climate of directed investigation and expertise advancement.

Freedom and Then some: Progressing to the Outside World

The progress to freedom is an essential stage in kangaroo parenthood. As joeys grow out of the pocket, they keep on depending on their moms for direction and security. Perceptions catch the continuous acquaintance of joeys with the outside climate, where they figure out how to scrounge for food and explore the intricacies of nature.

Male kangaroos, or boomers, likewise assume a vital part in kangaroo nurturing elements. They add to the wellbeing of the gathering, keeping a defensive edge around females and joeys. The agreeable idea of kangaroo nurturing stretches out past the mother-posterity dyad to incorporate more extensive social elements inside kangaroo networks.

Natural Difficulties and Variations

Kangaroo parenthood unfurls against the scenery of a dynamic and some of the time cruel climate. The illustrations from kangaroo mothers stretch out past sustaining ways of behaving to envelop the flexibility expected to flourish in different biological systems.

Dry season and Asset Shortage: Versatile Touching Examples

Dry season is a repetitive test in Australia, and kangaroo moms show versatility because of asset shortage. Perceptions feature changes in touching examples as kangaroos explore times of diminished water and food accessibility. The capacity to conform to the rhythmic movement of assets is a critical illustration from kangaroo parenthood, underscoring the significance of adaptability notwithstanding natural difficulties.

Human-Untamed life Clashes: Adjusting to Changing Scenes

As human improvement infringes on customary kangaroo natural surroundings, kangaroo moms grandstand their flexibility to evolving scenes. Perceptions in areas of human-untamed life struggle uncover how kangaroos alter their ways of behaving to explore urbanization. The flexibility of kangaroo parenthood becomes obvious as these marsupials adjust to new difficulties presented by human exercises.

Preservation Suggestions: Understanding and Safeguarding Kangaroo Parenthood

The illustrations from kangaroo parenthood hold suggestions for protection endeavors. Grasping the ways of behaving, transformations, and difficulties looked by kangaroo mothers is essential to informed preservation procedures. Saving their natural surroundings, relieving human-untamed life clashes, and recognizing the mind boggling elements of kangaroo nurturing add to the protection of these notorious marsupials.

3.1 Maternal Care and Bonding

Maternal consideration and holding address the foundation of supporting connections across the set of all animals, rising above species limits. From the mind boggling ways of behaving of warm blooded creatures to the dedicated guardianship of avian moms, the domain of parenthood reveals a rich embroidery of care, security, and close to home association. This investigation dives into the multi-layered parts of maternal consideration and holding, unwinding the natural establishments, conduct elements, and the getting through meaning of the maternal bond.

Natural Groundworks of Maternal Consideration

Hormonal Inclinations: The Maternal Diagram

The excursion of maternal consideration starts with organic inclinations encoded in the complex dance of chemicals. In vertebrates, the flood of oxytocin and prolactin during pregnancy and labor establishes the groundwork for maternal impulses. These chemicals start lactation as well as arrange the close to home reactions related with providing care.

Perceptions across species uncover the all inclusiveness of hormonal changes as an impetus for maternal ways of behaving. From the mammalian arrival of oxytocin during nursing to the avian flood of prolactin connected to egg-laying, the complex exchange of chemicals shapes the physiological background for the development of maternal consideration.

Neurobiological Pathways: Planning the Maternal Cerebrum

The brain hardware of maternal consideration is a multifaceted scene where different cerebrum districts fit to arrange sustaining ways of behaving. Concentrates on in well evolved creatures, especially rodents and primates, enlighten the brain processes associated with maternal consideration. The prefrontal cortex, amygdala, and nerve center team up to direct feelings, stress reactions, and maternal-baby holding.

The versatility of the maternal mind is a wonder, adjusting to the requests of providing care. Synapses, for example, dopamine and serotonin assume urgent parts in regulating state of mind and building up the joy related with maternal collaborations. Understanding the neurobiological underpinnings of maternal consideration uncovers the significant intricacy of the maternal mind's flexibility.

Conduct Elements of Maternal Consideration

Settling Ways of behaving: Making a Shelter for Posterity

The commencement of maternal consideration frequently appears in the careful development of homes or birthing destinations. Across different species, moms display inborn ways of behaving pointed toward establishing safe and supporting conditions for their posterity. From the intricate homes of birds to the painstakingly developed tunnels of warm blooded creatures, settling ways of behaving highlight the basic drive to give a safe house to the weak youthful.

Perceptions in the wild and controlled conditions uncover the accuracy and deliberateness behind settling ways of behaving. Moms put investment in making secure spaces that safeguard their posterity from hunters, climate limits, and possible dangers. Settling ceremonies act as a demonstration of the responsibility and premonition implanted in maternal consideration.

Preparing and Actual Consideration: Sustaining through Touch

Preparing ways of behaving, including the cautious cleaning and upkeep of posterity, are basic to maternal consideration in different taxa. Mammalian moms, from primates to ungulates, participate in complex preparing ceremonies that fill various needs. Past cleanliness, prepping encourages holding, manages internal heat level, and gives material solace.

The meaning of touch in maternal consideration reaches out past preparing to envelop actual closeness and soothing motions. Perceptions of moms supporting their babies, giving warmth through body contact, and answering the material necessities of their posterity feature the significant job of touch in the sustaining system. Maternal consideration, in this unique situation, turns into a tangible ensemble where contact is a language of consolation and association.

Taking care of Ways of behaving: Food and Association

In species with lactating moms, taking care of ways of behaving are a focal part of maternal consideration. The demonstration of nursing lays out a crucial connection among mother and posterity, giving fundamental supplements and cultivating a profound close to home association. Perceptions of nursing ways of behaving, from the cadenced hooking of mammalian youthful to the spewing forth of supplement rich food by avian moms, underscore the centrality of taking care of in maternal consideration.

The taking care of cycle isn't exclusively about sustenance; a unique connection hardens the connection among mother and posterity. Concentrates on breastfeeding in people highlight the mental and close to home advantages, with the arrival of holding chemicals, for example, oxytocin improving the maternal-newborn child association. Taking care of ways of behaving in this manner rise above the physiological demonstration of sustenance to turn into a significant articulation of maternal love and arrangement.

Watchfulness and Security: Guardianship Impulses

Maternal consideration stretches out to watchful ways of behaving pointed toward protecting posterity from possible dangers. Across the animals of the world collectively, moms show increased mindfulness, intense faculties, and cautious systems to guarantee the security of their young. From the careful attention of a lioness filtering the savannah for hunters to the essential cover utilized by settling birds, cautiousness is a sign of the guardianship impulses inborn in maternal consideration.

Perceptions of moms situating themselves between their posterity and possible risks, utilizing interruption strategies, or giving admonition calls highlight the profundity of maternal watchfulness. The defensive mantle expected by moms isn't just an impression of intuition yet a powerful reaction to the consistently present difficulties of the regular world.

The Close to home Scene of Maternal Holding

Acknowledgment and Connection: Fashioning Close to home Associations

Maternal consideration reaches out past instinctual ways of behaving to the domain of profound holding. In species where acknowledgment is essential, moms show amazing capacities to recognize and separate their posterity from others. The most common way of engraving, saw in birds and certain warm blooded creatures, is a piercing illustration of how early communications add to the development of solid and explicit securities.

Connection, a mental idea established in crafted by John Bowlby, is a significant component of maternal holding. The close to home association produced among mother and posterity is a dynamic and corresponding cycle. In warm blooded animals, concentrates on connection ways of behaving uncover the job of early encounters in molding the close to home scene of people, affecting social associations, and adding to generally speaking prosperity.

Correspondence and Language: Quiet Discoursed

Maternal consideration is frequently worked with by correspondence and language novel to every species. Without verbal correspondence, moms and posterity participate in quiet exchanges through a collection of vocalizations, non-verbal communication, and olfactory prompts. From the musical murmuring of a satisfied feline to the ultrasonic vocalizations of rodents, these specialized techniques build up the maternal-newborn child bond.

Perceptions of maternal correspondence reach out to the nuanced collaborations among moms and their posterity. In primates, for instance, looks, signals, and vocalizations assume significant parts in conveying feelings and building up friendly bonds. The unpredictable language of maternal consideration includes prompts that rise above the verbally expressed word, making a quiet yet significant exchange that fortifies the profound association among mother and posterity.

Social Learning and Demonstrating: Illustrations from the Maternal Figure

Maternal consideration stretches out to the domains of social learning and displaying, where the maternal figure turns into an instructor and guide. In species with expanded times of parental consideration, moms assume a focal part in granting fundamental basic instincts and social ways of behaving to their posterity. Perceptions of youthful creatures reflecting the activities of their moms, picking up hunting strategies, or copying social collaborations feature the meaning of maternal impact.

The idea of "maternal capital," authored by specialists, accentuates the important assets and information communicated from mother to posterity. In human social orders, the social transmission of customs, abilities, and values from mother to youngster mirrors the getting through effect of maternal direction.

The examples gained from the maternal figure become primary components that shape a person's versatile capacities and social discernment.

Difficulties to Maternal Consideration

Natural Tensions: Adjusting to Changing Circumstances

Maternal consideration faces difficulties as natural tensions, including environment changes, living space debasement, and asset shortage. Perceptions of moms adjusting to changing circumstances uncover the flexibility implanted in maternal senses. From transitory examples looking for reasonable settling locales to changes in taking care of ways of behaving during times of shortage, maternal consideration turns into a unique reaction to the difficulties presented by the climate.

Environmental change, specifically, acquaints new intricacies with maternal consideration. Increasing temperatures, modified precipitation examples, and natural surroundings interruptions expect moms to adjust their providing care procedures to guarantee the endurance of their posterity. The perceptions of such transformations highlight the versatile adaptability intrinsic in maternal consideration.

Human-Untamed life Clashes: Exploring Anthropogenic Difficulties

The infringement of human exercises into normal living spaces presents considerable difficulties to maternal consideration. Perceptions of natural life in areas of human-untamed life struggle feature the intricacies of exploring urbanization, deforestation, and living space discontinuity. Moms should battle with changed scenes, expanded human presence, and likely dangers to their posterity.

The transformation of maternal ways of behaving in light of human-natural life clashes uncovers the flexibility of parenthood despite anthropogenic difficulties. Whether it be changing settling destinations to stay away from human unsettling influence or modifying taking care of examples to limit experiences with metropolitan conditions, moms display a limit with regards to adaptable and key reactions

3.2 Nutritional Strategies Inside the Pouch

Inside the pocket, a novel domain of wholesome techniques unfurls as marsupials utilize a particular way to deal with supporting their young. This particular type of maternal provisioning is exemplified by marsupials like kangaroos, koalas, and wallabies. Inside the bounds of the pocket, an entrancing transaction of organic transformations, supplement rich emissions, and maternal consideration shapes the dietary scene for creating joeys. This investigation digs into the complexities of nourishing methodologies inside the pocket, disclosing the wonders of maternal provisioning in marsupials.

Natural Underpinnings of Pocket Sustenance

Exceptionally Lacking Youthful: The Pocket as a Defensive Sanctuary

Dissimilar to placental warm blooded creatures, marsupials bring forth exceptionally lacking youthful. Joeys, at the hour of birth, are in a beginning condition of improvement, looking like undeveloped organisms. The pocket fills in as a defensive safe house where these little, weak animals proceed with their development and early development. This remarkable conceptive system permits marsupials to shield their posterity in a pocket climate that is both supporting and secure.

Perceptions of marsupial moms uncover the fastidious consideration with which they take care of their joeys inside the pocket. The demonstration of directing the joeys from the birth waterway to the pocket and changing the pocket opening for taking care of mirrors the complicated organic dance of maternal consideration. The pocket, in this manner, turns into a microenvironment where healthful methodologies are custom fitted to meet the particular requirements of these exceptionally lacking youthful.

Lactation and Pocket Milk: A Unique Supplement Organization

One of the characterizing elements of nourishing systems inside the pocket is the development of pocket milk. Marsupials have mammary organs that discharge a specific type of milk custom-made to the formative phases of joeys. Pocket milk is unmistakable from the milk created during later progressive phases when joeys rise out of the pocket. The sythesis of pocket milk is powerfully controlled to address the developing nourishing prerequisites of joeys inside this restricted space.

Concentrates on pocket milk creation in different marsupials uncover a supplement rich mixture that incorporates proteins, fats, starches, and fundamental micronutrients. The exact equilibrium of these parts is coordinated to help fast development, resistant framework advancement, and in general wellbeing in the profoundly weak joeys. The uniqueness of pocket milk lies in its supplement creation as well as in the capacity of marsupial moms to change its substance in light of the changing necessities of their posterity.

Maternal Guideline of Pocket Milk Arrangement

Dynamic Changes in Supplement Proportions: Answering Development Stages

The nourishing prerequisites of joeys inside the pocket are not static. As they progress through various development stages, from early pocket life to the place of pocket rise, the supplement proportions in pocket milk go through unique changes. The capacity of marsupial moms to regulate the degrees of proteins, fats, and sugars guarantees that joeys get an ideal dietary profile at each transformative phase.

Perceptions of pocket milk arrangement in kangaroos, for instance, uncover higher protein content during the early pocket stage to help fast development and tissue improvement.

As joeys approach the mark of pocket rise, the fat substance increments to give the energy expected to the change to free taking care of. This unique guideline of supplement proportions embodies the complexities of maternal provisioning inside the pocket.

Immunological Elements in Pocket Milk: Building Early Resistance

Past macronutrients, pocket milk is enhanced with immunological variables pivotal for building early resistance in joeys. Marsupial moms move antibodies, resistant cells, and other protection components through their milk, giving a primary safeguard against microorganisms in the pocket climate. This inactive exchange of insusceptibility is essential during the beginning phases of pocket life when joeys are generally helpless to diseases.

Perceptions of resistant related parts in pocket milk feature the essential job of maternal provisioning in improving the strength of marsupial posterity. The capacity to give resistance through milk highlights the flexibility of marsupials to assorted ecological circumstances and the specific tensions of nature.

Difficulties and Transformations in Pocket Sustenance

Asset Shortage and Occasional Inconstancy: Exploring Nourishing Difficulties

Marsupials face difficulties related with asset shortage and occasional varieties in food accessibility. Pocket sustenance should adjust to these powerful circumstances, guaranteeing that joeys get satisfactory sustenance even notwithstanding natural difficulties. Perceptions of marsupials uncover versatile ways of behaving, for example, modified brushing designs, expanded rummaging effectiveness, and changes in maternal consideration methodologies to explore dietary vulnerabilities.

The capacity of marsupial moms to synchronize pocket sustenance with ecological circumstances features the versatility inborn in their conceptive systems. Nourishing moves become open doors for marsupials to feature their flexibility and ability to change maternal provisioning because of the always changing rhythms of nature.

Pocket Rise and Progress to Strong Food: Moving Healthful Standards

As joeys mature inside the pocket and move toward the mark of development, healthful techniques go through a significant shift. Pocket development denotes the progress to a stage where joeys continuously shift from dependence on pocket milk to free benefiting from strong food. Perceptions of this progress uncover a unique interchange between maternal direction, exploratory ways of behaving of joeys, and transformations to new dietary sources.

The most common way of weaning is a basic stage in pocket nourishment, where marsupial moms give direction and backing to joeys as they investigate and adjust to strong food varieties.

This progress features the adaptability of marsupial healthful procedures, taking into consideration a consistent shift from maternal provisioning to free scrounging.

Suggestions for Posterity Improvement and Endurance

Fast Development and Advancement: Outfitting Wholesome Assets

The wholesome techniques inside the pocket are finely tuned to help the fast development and improvement of marsupial joeys. The supplement rich pocket milk gives the fundamental structure blocks to tissues, organs, and generally physiological turn of events. Perceptions of joeys inside the pocket grandstand the amazing speed at which they develop, mirroring the proficiency of maternal provisioning in tackling wholesome assets.

The capacity to accomplish fast development inside the pocket is especially worthwhile in conditions where endurance relies on arriving at a specific size or formative stage rapidly. Marsupials show the transformative progress of this nourishing system in improving the possibilities posterity endurance in powerful and once in a while unforgiving environments.

Improved Strength to Natural Difficulties: Immunological Advantages

The immunological elements present in pocket milk give early resistance to marsupial joeys, improving their flexibility to natural difficulties. The latent exchange of antibodies and insusceptible cells outfits joeys with a fundamental protection against microorganisms, adding to their capacity to endure the afflictions of the pocket climate. Perceptions of marsupial posterity uncover a decreased weakness to diseases during the pocket stage, highlighting the immunological advantages of maternal provisioning.

The immunological benefits acquired through pocket nourishment have more extensive ramifications for the endurance of marsupial populaces. Upgraded flexibility to illnesses and contaminations adds to the general wellbeing and imperativeness of marsupial networks, impacting populace elements and biological communications.

Preservation and Exploration Suggestions

Figuring out Conceptive Methodologies: Informed Protection

The investigation of nourishing systems inside the pocket gives significant bits of knowledge into the regenerative techniques of marsupials. Grasping the complexities of maternal provisioning, pocket sustenance, and the versatile ways of behaving of marsupial moms illuminates preservation endeavors pointed toward safeguarding these special regenerative elements. Perceptions of wholesome transformations in light of natural difficulties add to the advancement of protection procedures that focus on the necessities of marsupial populaces.

Progressives can use information about nourishing methodologies inside the pocket to execute designated mediations, particularly despite anthropogenic dangers. Protecting the territories and biological circumstances that help ideal pocket nourishment becomes indispensable to defending the regenerative achievement and endurance of marsupial species.

Investigating Near Regenerative Science: Connecting Holes in Information

The assessment of wholesome techniques inside the pocket adds to the more extensive field of near regenerative science. Marsupials offer a one of a kind model for understanding the variety of conceptive techniques across mammalian taxa. Perceptions of pocket nourishment, lactation elements, and maternal consideration give similar information that improve how we might interpret the developmental directions molding conceptive variations in various species.

This near point of view has suggestions past marsupials, offering a focal point through which specialists can investigate the intermingling and dissimilarity of conceptive procedures across the collective of animals. Examples gained from marsupial wholesome methodologies might enlighten novel experiences into the intricacies of regenerative science, impacting research across assorted mammalian gatherings.

3.3 Protective Instincts and Teaching Moments

The complex dance of being a parent unfurls against the scenery of defensive impulses and showing minutes, a powerful embroidery woven by guardians across the animals of the world collectively. From the powerful vertebrates of the savannah to the sustaining birds in the treetops, the drive to safeguard and grant shrewdness to posterity is a widespread feature of nurturing. This investigation dives into the significant domains of defensive impulses and showing minutes, unwinding the developmental underpinnings, conduct elements, and persevering through meaning of these parental peculiarities.

Transformative Underpinnings of Defensive Senses
Endurance Basic: The Beginning of Defensive Senses

Defensive senses are well established in the transformative basic for species endurance. The battle for presence in the wild requires the defending of weak posterity from predation, ecological dangers, and different dangers. Perceptions across taxa uncover a range of defensive ways of behaving, going from careful watchfulness to forceful safeguard, as guardians endeavor to guarantee the prosperity and endurance of their descendants.

The sign of defensive impulses is formed by the natural specialties and life accounts of various species. In vertebrates, defensive ways of behaving frequently include the actual safeguarding of posterity, while in birds, key settling practices and alert calls act as defensive systems.

The variety of defensive impulses across the set of all animals confirms the versatility of nurturing procedures notwithstanding different natural difficulties.

Parental Venture and Regenerative Achievement

The idea of parental venture, presented by scientist Robert Trivers, explains the connection between defensive senses and conceptive achievement. Guardians contribute time, energy, and assets in raising posterity, and the level of parental venture differs among species. Defensive impulses address an unmistakable articulation of this venture, with guardians conveying a scope of systems to defend the hereditary heritage gave to the future.

Perceptions of defensive ways of behaving highlight the complex harmony between parental venture and the difficulties presented by the climate. The endurance of posterity isn't just a demonstration of the viability of defensive impulses yet additionally a proportion of regenerative achievement. Transformative tensions favor the advancement of defensive ways of behaving that upgrade the probability of posterity arriving at conceptive development, adding to the propagation of hereditary ancestries.

Conduct Elements of Defensive Senses

Cautiousness and Reconnaissance: The Careful attention of Being a parent

One of the principal indications of defensive impulses is the watchfulness shown by guardians. From well evolved creatures watching domains to birds roosted high in the trees, the careful focus of life as a parent is a consistent sentinel against likely dangers. The capacity to identify hunters, perceive ecological risks, and answer quickly to apparent dangers is a demonstration of the watchfulness imbued in defensive senses.

Perceptions of well evolved creatures, for example, lions and elephants uncover cooperative endeavors in reconnaissance, with guardians and other gathering individuals alternating to watch out for the environmental factors. In birds, sentinel ways of behaving include assigned people making the group aware of likely risks. This common obligation in carefulness features the social elements that frequently go with defensive impulses, encouraging agreeable endeavors to benefit posterity.

Actual Safeguard and Prevention: The Guardianship Impulse

Defensive impulses frequently raise to actual safeguard when posterity face up and coming dangers. The guardianship nature forces guardians to remain as considerable boundaries against hunters or adversaries, using actual ability and key posing to prevent possible risks. This nature is especially articulated in species where face to face conflicts with dangers are fundamental for the endurance of posterity.

In the wild, perceptions of moms safeguarding their young from hunters or fathers averting potential opponents grandstand the power of the guardianship impulse.

The eagerness to put oneself among posterity and danger, frequently at incredible individual gamble, highlights the conciliatory idea of defensive ways of behaving. The guardianship intuition is an impactful articulation of the profound close to home bond that pushes guardians to defy misfortune head-on for their descendants.

Versatile Reactions to Natural Difficulties

Defensive impulses are not static; they develop and adjust because of changing ecological circumstances. Guardians display a collection of versatile reactions to explore difficulties like food shortage, environment variances, and territory modifications. These versatile ways of behaving mirror the adaptability inborn in defensive impulses, permitting guardians to fit their reactions to the particular requirements and requests of their posterity.

Perceptions of creatures changing settling destinations because of environment changes, altering rummaging techniques during asset shortage, or migrating posterity to more secure territories in the midst of ecological pressure feature the unique idea of defensive senses. The ability to adjust is a significant part of effective nurturing, empowering species to flourish in different and frequently capricious environments.

Instructing Minutes: Supporting Through Direction

The Job of Showing in Posterity Advancement

Showing minutes are significant parts of parental direction, addressing amazing open doors for guardians to grant fundamental abilities, information, and ways of behaving to their posterity. In the wild, the transmission of abilities to survive is vital for the autonomous working and conceptive progress of posterity. Showing minutes overcome any barrier between parental security and the advancement of independence in the youthful.

Perceptions of showing minutes range a range of ways of behaving, from the exhibit of hunting strategies in carnivores to the coaching of flight abilities in birds. The purposeful and frequently monotonous nature of these communications mirrors the venture guardians make in setting up their posterity for the difficulties they will look in nature. Instructing turns into a dynamic and intuitive interaction that cultivates versatile capacities and improves the probability of posterity endurance.

Social Learning and Impersonation: The Force of Perception

Showing minutes frequently include social learning and impersonation, where posterity notice and copy the ways of behaving of their folks. The force of perception, combined with the capacity to impersonate, permits posterity to secure fundamental abilities and information through a course of experiential learning. This type of educating is especially conspicuous in species with broadened times of parental consideration.

In primates, for instance, perceptions of moms prepping, rummaging, and mingling give an outline to youthful people to gain proficiency with the complexities of social elements and methods for surviving. The course of social learning stretches out past the family unit to include more extensive local area associations, advancing the aggregate information pool of the gathering.

Experimentation Picking up: Building Flexibility Through Experience

Showing minutes frequently include a level of experimentation picking up, permitting posterity to fabricate flexibility and critical thinking abilities through direct insight. Guardians give open doors to their young to explore difficulties, decide, and gain from the two victories and disappointments. This type of experiential learning adds to the improvement of versatile ways of behaving and the sharpening of endurance impulses.

Perceptions of youthful creatures testing their actual cutoff points, investigating their surroundings, and taking part in play that mimics genuine situations epitomize the experimentation learning innate in educating minutes. The direction given by guardians permits posterity to foster a collection of abilities that will work well for them in adulthood, adding to their capacity to flourish in the intricacies of nature.

The Interaction Between Defensive Impulses and Educating Minutes

Cooperative Relationship: Sustaining Through Cautiousness and Direction

Defensive impulses and showing minutes are unpredictably entwined in the nurturing venture. The cooperative connection among watchfulness and direction makes an all encompassing way to deal with posterity care, where guardians safeguard their young from prompt dangers as well as furnish them with the devices required for long haul endurance. This transaction mirrors the complex idea of life as a parent, where defensive ways of behaving and showing minutes fit to support the future.

Perceptions of guardians keeping careful attention while at the same time taking part in showing minutes highlight the consistent joining of these parental elements. For instance, a lioness may cautiously examine the skyline for hunters while at the same time showing hunting strategies to her fledglings. This blend of defensive impulses and showing minutes represents the nuanced and versatile nature of parental consideration.

Slow Change to Autonomy: Adjusting Asylum and Independence

As posterity developed, the interaction between defensive impulses and showing minutes works with a continuous progress to freedom. The harmony between giving haven and encouraging independence turns into a fragile dance, with guardians steadily relaxing the reins as posterity get the right stuff and information expected to explore the difficulties of nature.

Perceptions of this change uncover an essential methodology by guardians to open their posterity to more prominent independence bit by bit. Showing minutes develop to incorporate situations that copy certifiable difficulties, planning posterity for the intricacies they will look as free people. A definitive objective is to outfit posterity with the strength and versatile capacities expected to flourish without the consistent sanctuary of parental security.

Difficulties to Parental Elements

Human-Natural life Struggle: Exploring Anthropogenic Difficulties

The many-sided equilibrium of defensive senses and showing minutes faces difficulties as human-untamed life clashes. As human exercises infringe into regular environments, the elements of parental consideration are disturbed, and species should explore novel dangers presented by urbanization, deforestation, and territory discontinuity. Perceptions of natural life in areas of human-natural life struggle feature the intricacies of adjusting defensive impulses and training minutes to alleviate the difficulties presented by anthropogenic exercises.

In certain occasions, the conflict between human exercises and untamed life prompts adjusted defensive ways of behaving, with guardians confronting expanded pressure and posterity experiencing new dangers. The need to explore these anthropogenic difficulties highlights the significance of protection endeavors that consider the intricacies of parental elements and look to alleviate the effect of human-untamed life clashes.

Environmental Change: Adjusting to Natural Movements

Environmental change acquaints extra layers of intricacy with parental elements, expecting species to adjust their defensive senses and helping minutes to moving natural circumstances. Perceptions of modified relocation designs, changed settling ways of behaving, and adjustments in showing systems feature the versatile reactions of guardians to the evolving environment.

The test presented by environmental change reaches out past prompt endurance to include the drawn out suitability of species. Defensive impulses and showing minutes should advance to address not just the quick dangers related with environmental change yet in addition the more extensive natural moves that influence the accessibility of assets and the appropriateness of territories for raising posterity.

Chapter 4

Kangaroo Dads - Unsung Heroes

In the huge and mind boggling universe of natural life nurturing, kangaroo fathers arise as overlooked yet truly great individuals, testing conventional thoughts of parental jobs in the collective of animals. While maternal consideration frequently takes the spotlight, kangaroo fathers assume a vital and unmistakable part in sustaining their posterity. This investigation dives into the extraordinary elements of kangaroo parenthood, unwinding the intricacies of their nurturing methodologies, the physiological transformations included, and the overlooked valor implanted in their commitments to the endurance and prosperity of their young.

Opposing Parental Generalizations: Kangaroo Fathers in Concentration
Maternal versus Fatherly Jobs: Breaking Generalizations in Nurturing

In the animals of the world collectively, parental jobs are frequently characteristically characterized, with moms normally bearing the essential obligations of care, assurance, and sustenance. Nonetheless, kangaroo fathers resist these generalizations, testing the customary account of fatherly jobs in nurturing. Their dynamic association in raising posterity and their remarkable commitments to the nuclear family illustrate parenthood in nature.

Perceptions of kangaroo fathers participating in providing care ways of behaving, conveying and shielding their young, and effectively partaking in the childhood of joeys feature the versatile adaptability of parental jobs. The obscured lines among maternal and fatherly obligations in kangaroo families highlight the unique idea of nurturing systems, where each parent assumes an imperative part in guaranteeing the progress of the future.

Shared Liabilities in Kangaroo Families

Kangaroo fathers effectively share liabilities with moms in raising their young, making a cooperative and helpful relational peculiarity. Not at all like a few animal groups where fathers might have restricted contribution in nurturing, kangaroo fathers contribute essentially to the prosperity of joeys. The common obligations include security, warm guideline, and direction during basic formative stages.

Perceptions of kangaroo families uncover occurrences where fathers effectively take part in prepping, giving a safe pocket climate, and, surprisingly, captivating in play with their posterity. This common obligation to nurturing features the many-sided social designs inside kangaroo networks, testing assumptions about the division of work among moms and fathers in nature.

Physiological Variations of Kangaroo Fathers

Pouchless Nurturing: The Developmental Benefit of a Special Technique

Not at all like numerous marsupials, male kangaroos come up short on pocket, a trademark highlight normally connected with maternal consideration. This shortfall of a pocket difficulties conventional assumptions for marsupial nurturing and highlights the extraordinary developmental procedure took on by kangaroo fathers. The pouchless nurturing approach includes elective systems for shielding and sustaining their young.

Perceptions of kangaroo fathers without pockets uncover the usage of various methodologies to give care to their posterity. Fathers utilize areas of strength for them to make a steady and secure pocket like climate, permitting joeys to take shelter and get insurance. The transformative variation of pouchless nurturing mirrors the genius and versatility innate in kangaroo fathers.

Tail as a Strong Device: Kangaroo Fathers' Brilliant Nurturing Help

The tail of a kangaroo fills in as a flexible and strong device without a pocket. Kangaroo fathers utilize their tails for equilibrium and portability as well as for the purpose of making a solid space for their joeys. The tail turns into a dynamic and versatile expansion of fatherly providing care, exhibiting the creativity of kangaroo fathers in giving a supporting climate to their posterity.

Perceptions of kangaroo fathers utilizing their tails to support and support joeys, particularly during weak transformative phases, feature the multifunctional job of this member. The tail, when considered fundamentally a device for bouncing and equilibrium, turns into a significant instrument in the tool stash of kangaroo fathers, adding to the progress of their nurturing procedures.

Warm Guideline: Kangaroo Fathers as Living Hatcheries

Without any a conventional pocket, kangaroo fathers assume a fundamental part in warm guideline for their joeys. Keeping up with ideal internal heat level is basic for the endurance and prosperity of marsupial youthful, and kangaroo fathers grandstand their capacity to go about as living hatcheries for their posterity. The nearby body contact and safe house given by fathers add to the warm solace and improvement of joeys.

Perceptions of kangaroo fathers changing their situations to safeguard joeys from unforgiving weather patterns or involving their bodies as a defensive boundary during colder periods highlight the meaning of fatherly commitments to the warm prosperity of their young. This versatile way to deal with warm guideline is a demonstration of the creativity of kangaroo fathers in giving a favorable climate to the development and improvement of their joeys.

Parental Venture: The Cost of Kangaroo Parenthood

Enthusiastic Expenses of Kangaroo Parenthood: Adjusting Care and Endurance

Kangaroo parenthood accompanies its own arrangement of fiery expenses, as fathers focus profoundly on giving consideration to their posterity. The harmony between parental speculation and individual endurance is a sensitive one, and kangaroo fathers explore this dynamic by decisively dispensing their energy to guarantee the prosperity of their young.

Perceptions of kangaroo fathers taking part in dynamic providing care ways of behaving, for example, conveying joeys for broadened periods, feature the physical and metabolic requests of fatherly obligations. The obligation to parental speculation, notwithstanding the possible dangers to individual endurance, highlights the developmental significance of the pretended by kangaroo fathers in the conceptive outcome of their species.

Influence on Friendly Elements: Kangaroo People group and Family Bonds

The dynamic association of kangaroo fathers in nurturing adds to the perplexing social elements inside kangaroo networks. Family bonds are fortified as the two guardians effectively take part in raising and safeguarding their young. The cooperative endeavors of kangaroo mothers and fathers establish a strong climate where posterity get extensive consideration, cultivating the flexibility and versatility of the whole nuclear family.

Perceptions of kangaroo families communicating, playing, and rummaging together feature the positive effect of fatherly commitments on the attachment of the gathering. The social texture woven by shared parental obligations supports the feeling of local area inside kangaroo populaces, displaying the interconnectedness of individual jobs in the more extensive setting of day to day life.

Formative Stages: Kangaroo Fathers in real life

Infant Joey Care: The Job of Kangaroo Fathers all along

The association of kangaroo fathers in nurturing starts with the consideration of infant joeys. In the underlying progressive phases, when joeys are at their generally powerless, kangaroo fathers effectively take part in establishing a solid climate for their posterity.

The tail turns into a urgent device for shielding and supporting the little joeys, offering them insurance and a feeling that all is well with the world.

Perceptions of kangaroo fathers changing their tails to support infant joeys, guaranteeing their security and solace, embody the active way to deal with nurturing displayed all along. The fatherly commitment during this basic stage adds to the endurance and prosperity of joeys, establishing the groundwork for the solid bonds that will create among fathers and their posterity.

Conveying and Scavenging: Kangaroo Fathers as Versatile Nurseries

As joeys develop and turn out to be more versatile, kangaroo fathers accept the job of portable nurseries, conveying their posterity with them as they scavenge for food. The tail and the solid rear appendages of fathers become instrumental in giving a protected and stable roost for joeys, permitting them to notice and learn while being moved.

Perceptions of kangaroo fathers bouncing with joeys settled against their bodies grandstand the productivity of this versatile nurturing technique. The nearness among fathers and joeys during scrounging undertakings works with proceeded with insurance as well as opens posterity to important growth opportunities about food sources and natural signs.

Educating Minutes: Kangaroo Fathers as Advisers for Autonomy

As joeys progress to additional free transformative phases, kangaroo fathers assume a critical part in giving direction and working with opportunities for growth. Showing minutes unfurl as fathers open their posterity to various parts of the climate, like rummaging procedures, social collaborations, and route abilities. The tail, when a strong device, turns into an instrument of direction as fathers support investigation and freedom in their young.

Perceptions of kangaroo fathers persistently permitting joeys to explore different avenues regarding their environmental factors, jump close by them, and bit by bit become more independent highlight the supporting direction gave during this basic stage. Kangaroo fathers become guides, cultivating the advancement of versatile ways of behaving and abilities to survive that will work well for their posterity in nature.

Difficulties and Variations: The Dangers of Kangaroo Parenthood

Predation Dangers: Adjusting Insurance and Openness

The job of kangaroo fathers in nurturing accompanies intrinsic dangers, especially regarding predation. As fathers effectively convey and really focus on their young, the weakness of both parent and posterity increments. Perceptions of kangaroo fathers exploring the sensitive harmony between giving security and uncovering themselves and their joeys to potential hunters shed light on the difficulties of parenthood in nature.

The versatile methodologies utilized by kangaroo fathers to relieve predation gambles incorporate cautiousness, vital situating, and quick reactions to likely dangers. The consistent mindfulness showed by fathers mirrors their obligation to the security of their posterity, even despite the hazards related with parental consideration.

Asset Shortage: Giving in Testing Conditions

Kangaroo fathers should battle with the difficulties of asset shortage, particularly during times of dry season or food deficiencies. As essential foragers answerable for both self-food and supporting their young, fathers face the overwhelming errand of giving in conditions where assets might be restricted. Perceptions of kangaroo fathers changing searching examples, investigating new regions, and adjusting their systems in light of ecological vacillations feature the versatility and flexibility expected to explore asset challenges.

The effect of asset shortage stretches out past the quick requirements of fathers to the general prosperity of kangaroo populaces. The capacity of fathers to explore and defeat these difficulties adds to the endurance and conceptive progress of their species.

Protection Suggestions: Perceiving the Job of Kangaroo Fathers

Saving Natural surroundings Trustworthiness: Guaranteeing Kangaroo Father Achievement

Protection endeavors pointed toward saving kangaroo populaces should consider the one of a kind commitments of kangaroo fathers to conceptive achievement. Perceiving the significance of fathers in the general elements of kangaroo families highlights the need to focus on natural surroundings honesty. Safeguarding regular habitats with adequate assets and reasonable circumstances is essential for supporting the nurturing techniques of kangaroo fathers and guaranteeing the proceeded with progress of their posterity.

Perceptions of kangaroo fathers flourishing in undisturbed natural surroundings feature the relationship between's ecological wellbeing and conceptive achievement. Protection drives that focus on natural surroundings conservation and rebuilding contribute not exclusively to the prosperity of kangaroo fathers yet additionally to the general strength of marsupial populaces.

Alleviating Human-Natural life Struggle: Concurrence Systems

As human exercises infringe into regular environments, kangaroo populaces face the difficulties of human-untamed life struggle. Preservation endeavors should incorporate systems for moderating struggle and encouraging conjunction among people and kangaroo families. Perceptions of kangaroo fathers adjusting to metropolitan conditions and exploring human presence highlight the flexibility of fathers notwithstanding anthropogenic difficulties.

Carrying out measures like natural surroundings hallways, instructive projects, and mindful land use arranging can add to lessening struggle and making spaces where kangaroo fathers can proceed with their vital job in nurturing without unnecessary aggravation.

4.1 The Role of Male Kangaroos in Parenting

In the rambling scenes of the Australian outback, where notable marsupials meander aimlessly, the job of male kangaroos in nurturing arises as a captivating and frequently ignored part of natural life conduct. Generally, maternal consideration becomes the overwhelming focus in conversations of nurturing among marsupials, yet male kangaroos, or boomers, assume a pivotal part in sustaining the future. This investigation dives into the multi-layered liabilities and extraordinary commitments of male kangaroos in nurturing, revealing insight into their providing care ways of behaving, physiological variations, and the more extensive ramifications for the endurance and prosperity of kangaroo populaces.

Breaking Generalizations: Male Kangaroos in the Parental Spotlight

Scattering Ideas of Latent Life as a parent

In the domain of marsupials, maternal consideration has for quite some time been the point of convergence of logical request and public interest. The picture of a mother kangaroo with a joey settled in her pocket has become inseparable from marsupial nurturing. Nonetheless, the story of uninvolved parenthood for male kangaroos is bit by bit being tested, as perceptions uncover a more dynamic and involved job in the childhood of posterity.

In opposition to generalizations of male kangaroos as single and separated guardians, studies have shown that they effectively add to the consideration and security of their young. Perceptions of male kangaroos associating with joeys, giving haven, and taking part in different providing care ways of behaving challenge assumptions and highlight the significance of figuring out the intricacies of kangaroo relational peculiarities.

Shared Parental Obligations

In kangaroo families, parental obligations are not unbendingly split among moms and fathers. Both male and female kangaroos effectively take part in raising and defending their young, making a cooperative way to deal with nurturing. The common obligations envelop viewpoints like security, warm guideline, and direction during various formative stages.

Perceptions of male kangaroos participating in prepping, conveying joeys, and partaking in play with their posterity feature the agreeable idea of nurturing inside kangaroo networks.

This common obligation to the prosperity of joeys challenges customary thoughts of orientation explicit jobs in marsupial families, underscoring the ease and versatility of parental obligations.

Physiological Variations: Fitting Nurturing to the Kangaroo Way of life
Pouchless Nurturing: The Transformative Methodology of Male Kangaroos

One of the unmistakable highlights of male kangaroos in nurturing is the shortfall of a pocket, a trademark characteristic regularly connected with marsupial moms. Not at all like females, male kangaroos miss the mark on specific physical construction to give a safe pocket climate to their young. This pouchless nurturing approach requires elective techniques for shielding and supporting posterity.

Perceptions of male kangaroos utilizing major areas of strength for them to make a steady and secure space for joeys embody the versatile idea of pouchless nurturing. The tail turns into a flexible instrument, offering help and sanctuary for youthful joeys during weak progressive phases. The development of pouchless nurturing features the genius and versatility inborn in male kangaroos as they tailor their providing care to the extraordinary difficulties of the kangaroo way of life.

Tail as a Nurturing Device: Supporting and Supporting Joeys

The tail of a male kangaroo fills in as a dynamic and steady device without a trace of a pocket. Perceptions of male kangaroos utilizing their tails to support and support joeys feature the flexibility of this extremity in nurturing. The tail turns into an expansion of fatherly providing care, offering joeys a solid roost and adding to their general wellbeing and solace.

The tail of a male kangaroo isn't simply a method for impetus during bouncing however a multifunctional instrument that guides in nurturing. Whether giving a steady stage to joeys to rest or effectively partaking in the direction of posterity, the tail exhibits the cunning transformations of male kangaroos to satisfy their nurturing obligations.

Warm Guideline: Male Kangaroos as Living Hatcheries

Keeping up with ideal internal heat level is pivotal for the endurance and improvement of marsupial joeys. Without a pocket, male kangaroos assume an imperative part in warm guideline for their posterity. The nearby body contact among fathers and joeys gives a living hatchery impact, guaranteeing that youthful marsupials are shielded from temperature variances in the outside climate.

Perceptions of male kangaroos changing their situations to safeguard joeys from outrageous weather patterns or involving their bodies as a defensive hindrance during colder periods highlight the significance of fatherly commitments to the warm prosperity of their young.

This physiological variation features the unique idea of male kangaroo nurturing, where fathers effectively participate in keeping up with the ideal circumstances for the development and advancement of their posterity.

Parental Speculation: The Vigorous Expenses of Parenthood
Adjusting Parental Speculation and Individual Endurance

The job of male kangaroos in nurturing accompanies innate vivacious expenses. As fathers effectively participate in providing care ways of behaving, convey joeys for broadened periods, and take part in the childhood of posterity, they should explore the sensitive harmony between parental venture and individual endurance. The obligation to giving consideration to youthful joeys requires critical physical and metabolic assets, influencing the general energy financial plan of male kangaroos.

Perceptions of male kangaroos taking part in dynamic nurturing, notwithstanding the possible dangers to their own prosperity, feature the devotion and penance engaged with parenthood. The capacity to offset parental speculation with individual endurance is a basic part of male kangaroo nurturing, adding to the conceptive achievement and long haul endurance of their species.

Social Elements: Reinforcing Family Bonds

The dynamic association of male kangaroos in nurturing adds to the complex social elements inside kangaroo networks. Family bonds are fortified as the two guardians effectively partake in raising and safeguarding their young. The cooperative endeavors of male and female kangaroos establish a strong climate where posterity get complete consideration, encouraging the versatility and flexibility of the whole nuclear family.

Perceptions of kangaroo families communicating, playing, and scavenging together feature the positive effect of fatherly commitments on the union of the gathering. The social texture woven by shared parental obligations builds up the feeling of local area inside kangaroo populaces, displaying the interconnectedness of individual jobs in the more extensive setting of everyday life.

Formative Stages: Male Kangaroos as Parental figures Through Time

Infant Joey Care: The Job of Male Kangaroos all along

Male kangaroos effectively take part under the watchful eye of infant joeys, adding to their prosperity from the earliest transformative phases. The shortfall of a conventional pocket doesn't lessen the job of fathers in establishing a safe climate for their young. Perceptions of male kangaroos changing their tails to support and support infant joeys epitomize the involved way to deal with nurturing showed all along.

The fatherly commitment during the basic period of infant care establishes the groundwork for the solid bonds that will foster between male kangaroos and their posterity. The help given by fathers during this weak stage adds to the endurance and fruitful improvement of joeys in nature.

Conveying and Scrounging: Male Kangaroos as Portable Nurturers

As joeys develop and turn out to be more portable, male kangaroos accept the job of versatile nurturers, conveying their posterity with them as they search for food. The tail and the solid rear appendages of fathers become instrumental in giving a safe and stable roost for joeys, permitting them to notice, learn, and participate in the general climate.

Perceptions of male kangaroos jumping with joeys settled against their bodies exhibit the productivity of this portable nurturing methodology. The closeness among fathers and joeys during searching endeavors works with proceeded with security as well as opens posterity to important opportunities for growth about food sources and ecological signals.

Educating Minutes: Male Kangaroos as Advisers for Freedom

As joeys progress to additional free transformative phases, male kangaroos assume a urgent part in giving direction and working with growth opportunities. Showing minutes unfurl as fathers open their posterity to various parts of the climate, like rummaging procedures, social connections, and route abilities. The tail, when a steady device, turns into an instrument of direction as fathers empower investigation and freedom in their young.

Perceptions of male kangaroos persistently permitting joeys to explore different avenues regarding their environmental factors, jump close by them, and continuously become more independent highlight the supporting direction gave during this basic stage. Male kangaroos become guides, cultivating the improvement of versatile ways of behaving and abilities to survive that will work well for their posterity in nature.

Difficulties and Transformations: The Risks of Kangaroo Parenthood

Predation Dangers: Exploring the Difficult exercise

The job of male kangaroos in nurturing accompanies innate dangers, especially regarding predation. As fathers effectively convey and really focus on their young, the weakness of both parent and posterity increments. Perceptions of male kangaroos exploring the fragile harmony between giving assurance and uncovering themselves and their joeys to potential hunters shed light on the difficulties of parenthood in nature.

The versatile techniques utilized by male kangaroos to relieve predation gambles incorporate carefulness, key situating, and quick reactions to likely dangers.

The consistent mindfulness displayed by fathers mirrors their obligation to the wellbeing of their posterity, even notwithstanding the dangers related with parental consideration.

Asset Shortage: Giving in Testing Conditions

Male kangaroos should battle with the difficulties of asset shortage, particularly during times of dry season or food deficiencies. As essential foragers answerable for both self-food and supporting their young, fathers face the overwhelming errand of giving in conditions where assets might be restricted. Perceptions of male kangaroos changing scrounging designs, investigating new regions, and adjusting their techniques in light of ecological variances feature the versatility and flexibility expected to explore asset challenges.

The effect of asset shortage reaches out past the quick requirements of fathers to the general prosperity of kangaroo populaces. The capacity of male kangaroos to explore and conquer these difficulties adds to the endurance and conceptive progress of their species.

Preservation Suggestions: Perceiving the Vital Job of Male Kangaroos

Saving Living space Uprightness: A Key to Kangaroo Father Achievement

Protection endeavors pointed toward saving kangaroo populaces should consider the remarkable commitments of male kangaroos to conceptive achievement. Perceiving the significance of fathers in the general elements of kangaroo families highlights the need to focus on natural surroundings honesty. Safeguarding regular habitats with adequate assets and reasonable circumstances is pivotal for supporting the nurturing techniques of male kangaroos and guaranteeing the proceeded with outcome of their posterity.

Perceptions of male kangaroos flourishing in undisturbed living spaces feature the connection between's ecological wellbeing and regenerative achievement. Protection drives that focus on living space safeguarding and rebuilding contribute not exclusively to the prosperity of male kangaroos yet additionally to the general strength of marsupial populaces.

Alleviating Human-Natural life Struggle: Methodologies for Conjunction

As human exercises infringe into regular environments, kangaroo populaces face the difficulties of human-untamed life struggle. Preservation endeavors should incorporate systems for alleviating struggle and encouraging concurrence among people and kangaroo families. Perceptions of male kangaroos adjusting to metropolitan conditions and exploring human presence highlight the strength of fathers notwithstanding anthropogenic difficulties.

Executing measures like natural surroundings passageways, instructive projects, and dependable land use arranging can add to lessening struggle and making spaces where male kangaroos can proceed with their urgent job in nurturing without unnecessary aggravation.

4.2 Cooperative Parenting Dynamics

In the immense embroidery of the animals of the world collectively, helpful nurturing elements stand apart as an exceptional peculiarity, testing conventional thoughts of single and individualistic nurturing. While the picture of a solitary parent really focusing on its posterity is profoundly imbued in how we might interpret the wild, helpful nurturing reveals an alternate story — one of cooperation, shared liabilities, and public endeavors. This investigation digs into the interesting universe of helpful nurturing elements, analyzing the species that epitomize this methodology, the advantages it gives, and the developmental ramifications for the endurance of posterity.

Challenging the Lone Model: Species that Embrace Collaboration

Social Carnivores: Wolves and African Wild Canines

Among the most notable instances of agreeable nurturing are social carnivores, especially wolves and African wild canines. In these species, nurturing is a common undertaking including various grown-ups, frequently related people, cooperating to guarantee the prosperity and endurance of the pack's posterity.

Perceptions of wolf packs uncover an organized order where both alpha and beta people take part in raising little guys. Grown-up wolves participate in exercises like hunting, giving security, and in any event, spewing food to take care of the youthful. The cooperative endeavors inside the pack improve the possibilities of endurance for the whole gathering, making areas of strength for a unit.

African wild canines also display agreeable nurturing, with an alpha rearing pair upheld by different grown-ups in the pack. Non-rearing people add to the consideration, security, and instruction of the little guys. This helpful methodology disperses the weight of nurturing as well as supports the social bonds that are essential for the progress of the whole pack.

Avian Collaboration: The Sentinel Framework in Helpful Raisers

In the avian domain, agreeable nurturing is exemplified by specific bird species known as helpful reproducers. These birds take part in an exceptional framework where different people, frequently non-reproducing assistants, help a rearing pair in raising their posterity.

One astounding model is the Florida scour jay, where posterity from past reproducing seasons stay behind to help their folks in focusing on new little birds. These assistants add to settle safeguard, scrounging, and in any event, taking care of the youthful, upgrading the generally speaking regenerative outcome of the reproducing pair.

Another striking model is the great pixie wren, where non-reproducing people help the predominant rearing pair. These partners assume an essential part in safeguarding homes, scavenging for food, and giving consideration to the chicks. The helpful rearing framework in these avian species exhibits the benefits of shared liabilities in raising posterity.

Advantages of Agreeable Nurturing

Expanded Posterity Endurance: Strength in Numbers

One of the essential benefits of agreeable nurturing elements is the improved probability of posterity endurance. In species where different grown-ups add to providing care, there is a more prominent ability to give security, scavenge for food, and shield against hunters. This cooperative exertion makes a security net for the weak youthful, essentially working on their possibilities arriving at development.

In friendly carnivores like wolves, the aggregate hunting ability of the pack guarantees a steady food supply for the developing puppies. Likewise, in agreeable rearing birds, the joined endeavors of different people lead to more effective home guard and improved provisioning of nourishment for the little birds.

Asset Sharing and Division of Work

Helpful nurturing considers a division of work among people, upgrading the utilization of accessible assets. In species where providing care liabilities are shared, various grown-ups can have some expertise in unambiguous assignments, whether it be hunting, home guard, or preparing. This specialization upgrades in general proficiency, guaranteeing that every part of nurturing gets committed consideration.

For instance, in meerkats, a helpful mammalian animal categories, people alternate going about as sentinels, looking for hunters while others rummage. This division of work permits the gathering to apportion assets successfully, adding to the endurance and prosperity of the whole local area.

Social Holding and Learning Amazing open doors

Helpful nurturing major areas of strength for encourages securities inside a gathering, making a feeling of local area and common reliance. Posterity brought up in such a climate not just advantage from the providing care endeavors of numerous grown-ups yet additionally have the chance to gain fundamental abilities from a different arrangement of people.

In African wild canine packs, youthful little guys take part in play and social cooperations with their folks as well as with different grown-ups in the gathering. This openness to various providing care styles and ways of behaving adds to the advancement of versatile abilities urgent for endurance in nature.

Developmental Ramifications: Helpful Nurturing as a Versatile System

Wellness Advantages and Comprehensive Wellness Hypothesis

The idea of comprehensive wellness, presented by scientist W.D. Hamilton, gives a hypothetical system to grasping the developmental benefits of helpful nurturing. Comprehensive wellness considers a person's own conceptive accomplishment as well as the regenerative outcome of family members with shared hereditary material.

Agreeable nurturing, by improving the endurance and conceptive progress of related people, lines up with the standards of comprehensive wellness. In species where connection assumes a huge part, people aiding the nurturing system add to the proliferation of shared hereditary material, at last expanding the comprehensive wellness of the gathering.

Variations to Natural Difficulties

Helpful nurturing should be visible as a versatile reaction to explicit natural difficulties. In natural surroundings where assets are scant, predation pressure is high, or ecological circumstances are erratic, the cooperative endeavors of numerous people increment the versatility and flexibility of a populace.

For example, in meerkat populaces possessing bone-dry conditions, the division of work and shared liabilities add to the productive utilization of restricted assets and improve the's gathering skill to adapt to the difficulties of their dry environmental elements.

Difficulties and Impediments of Agreeable Nurturing
Struggle and Rivalry Inside Gatherings

While helpful nurturing offers various advantages, it isn't without challenges. Now and again, struggle and contest might emerge inside gatherings, particularly when assets are restricted. Rivalry for rearing open doors, admittance to food, or the opportunity to really focus on posterity can prompt strain and progressive battles among bunch individuals.

In specific agreeable reproducing bird species, clashes might emerge between the rearing pair and partners over the portion of assets or parental obligations. These contentions can affect the general congruity of the gathering and, in outrageous cases, lead to the ejection of specific people.

Reliance on Gathering Strength

The outcome of helpful nurturing procedures is much of the time dependent upon the steadiness and attachment of the gathering. Interruptions, like the deficiency of key people or the breakdown of social bonds, can significantly affect the adequacy of agreeable nurturing. At times, the disappointment of agreeable endeavors might bring about diminished posterity endurance and conceptive achievement.

For instance, in helpful reproducers like the magnificent pixie wren, disturbances in the social construction or the deficiency of key people can affect the general working of the gathering and its capacity to effectively raise posterity.

4.3 Unique Contributions of Kangaroo Fathers

The picture of a supporting guardian is frequently connected with moms, yet in the marsupial world, kangaroo fathers challenge conventional generalizations of uninvolved parenthood. In the tremendous scenes of Australia, male kangaroos, or boomers, assume novel and fundamental parts in nurturing that stretch out a long ways past the normally seen picture of moms with joeys in their pockets. This investigation reveals the unmistakable commitments of kangaroo fathers, revealing insight into their versatile ways of behaving, imparted liabilities to moms, and the multifaceted elements that describe kangaroo everyday life.

Pouchless Nurturing: The Customized Approach of Kangaroo Fathers

One of the most distinctive elements of kangaroo fathers is their pouchless nurturing technique. Dissimilar to female kangaroos furnished with specific pockets for protecting their young, male kangaroos come up short on physical construction. In any case, this nonappearance doesn't reduce their nurturing commitments. All things being equal, kangaroo fathers have developed one of a kind transformations to make up for the absence of a pocket.

The tail, a strong and solid extremity, turns into a flexible device for kangaroo fathers. Perceptions uncover guys utilizing their tails to make a safe and stable roost for joeys, supporting and supporting them as they bounce. This tail-as-pocket approach grandstands the creativity of kangaroo fathers in giving a defensive climate to their posterity, in spite of the shortfall of a conventional pocket.

Warm Guideline: Kangaroo Fathers as Living Hatcheries

Keeping up with ideal internal heat level is pivotal for the endurance and advancement of marsupial joeys. Without a pocket, male kangaroos expect the job of living hatcheries for their young. Close body contact among fathers and joeys fills in as a characteristic system for warm guideline, shielding the weak posterity from temperature vacillations in the outside climate.

Perceptions of kangaroo fathers changing their situations to safeguard joeys from outrageous weather patterns or involving their bodies as a defensive obstruction during colder periods highlight the significance of fatherly commitments to the warm prosperity of their young. This one of a kind type of warm guideline features the versatility of kangaroo fathers to the difficulties of pouchless nurturing.

Portable Nurturers: Kangaroo Fathers in real life

As joeys develop and turn out to be more portable, kangaroo fathers progress into the job of versatile nurturers. The solid rear appendages and hearty tails of guys become instrumental in giving a protected and stable roost for joeys during rummaging campaigns. Perceptions of kangaroo fathers jumping with joeys settled against their bodies grandstand the effectiveness of this versatile nurturing system.

The closeness among fathers and joeys during scrounging guarantees proceeded with security as well as opens posterity to significant opportunities for growth about food sources and natural prompts. This active way to deal with nurturing by kangaroo fathers adds to the general turn of events and schooling of their young in nature.

Advisers for Freedom: Kangaroo Fathers as Coaches

As joeys progress to additional free transformative phases, kangaroo fathers assume a vital part in directing their posterity towards independence. Showing minutes unfurl as fathers open their young to various parts of the climate, including searching strategies, social connections, and route abilities. The tail, when a strong device, turns into an instrument of direction as kangaroo fathers support investigation and freedom in their joeys.

Perceptions of male kangaroos quietly permitting joeys to explore different avenues regarding their environmental elements, jump close by them, and step by step become more independent highlight the supporting direction gave during this basic stage. Kangaroo fathers become guides, encouraging the improvement of versatile ways of behaving and abilities to survive that will work well for their posterity in nature.

Difficulties and Variations: The Risks of Kangaroo Parenthood

While kangaroo fathers effectively participate in nurturing, their jobs accompany inborn difficulties. Predation chances, asset shortage, and the difficult exercise of giving assurance while uncovering themselves and their young to the climate are consistent contemplations for kangaroo fathers.

Perceptions of fathers exploring the fragile harmony between safeguarding their posterity and relieving predation gambles with shed light on the difficulties of parenthood in nature. The versatile techniques utilized by kangaroo fathers, from cautiousness to vital situating, mirror their obligation to the wellbeing and endurance of their young.

Preservation Suggestions: Perceiving the Pivotal Job of Kangaroo Fathers

Understanding the remarkable commitments of kangaroo fathers has significant ramifications for preservation endeavors. Perceiving the essential job of guys in kangaroo families highlights the need to focus on living space safeguarding and rebuilding. Safeguarding regular habitats with adequate assets is significant for supporting the nurturing procedures of kangaroo fathers and guaranteeing the proceeded with outcome of their posterity.

Perceptions of kangaroo fathers flourishing in undisturbed living spaces feature the connection between's natural wellbeing and regenerative achievement. Protection drives that focus on the safeguarding of kangaroo populaces should recognize the multi-layered commitments of the two moms and fathers to the general elements of marsupial families.

Chapter 5

Kangaroo Parenting and Human Parenthood

Nurturing, a widespread peculiarity that rises above species limits, shows fascinating varieties and similitudes across the set of all animals. While the experience of being a parent among people is well established in social, close to home, and mental aspects, investigating the nurturing techniques of different species offers important bits of knowledge and viewpoints. This extensive assessment dives into the universe of kangaroo nurturing, disentangling its remarkable elements, and draws matches with the complicated embroidery of human being a parent. From regenerative procedures to providing care ways of behaving, this investigation looks to enlighten the common strings that wind through the apparently different domains of kangaroos and people.

Regenerative Methodologies: Marsupials and Vertebrates Revealed

Gestational Contrasts: In Pocket versus In Utero

The underpinning of nurturing starts with conceptive methodologies, and in this domain, kangaroos and people set out on disparate ways. Kangaroos, as marsupials, embrace a novel methodology known as pocket nurturing. Not at all like people, kangaroos have a concise growth period, with moms bringing forth somewhat lacking posterity. The minuscule, untimely joeys slither into the mother's pocket, where they proceed to create and get sustenance.

Conversely, people, as placental well evolved creatures, experience a delayed growth period inside the mother's belly. Human posterity go through broad improvement in utero, depending on a placental association for supplement trade and security. The unique conceptive methodologies feature the versatility of vertebrates to different biological specialties and natural difficulties.

Pocket Nurturing and Human Outset: A Near Focal point

The idea of kangaroo pocket nurturing offers a special viewpoint while thinking about human earliest stages. While human babies are supported in the arms of their parental figures, kangaroo joeys track down shelter inside the pocket — a particular outer belly. The pocket gives a solid and supporting climate for kangaroo posterity, working with their development and improvement outside the limits of the belly.

In the human setting, the providing care climate is more externalized, including the utilization of bunks, transporters, and other strong designs. Be that as it may, the basic rule stays consistent: the requirement for a defensive and sustaining space during the weak phases of early stages. The similar investigation highlights the meaning of establishing favorable conditions for the early improvement of posterity across species.

Providing care Ways of behaving: Bits of knowledge from Kangaroo Pocket Nurturing

Maternal and Fatherly Commitments: A Fair Methodology

In kangaroo families, providing care isn't exclusively the space of moms; fathers, or boomers, assume dynamic parts in the childhood of their young. Kangaroo fathers take part in fitting and giving a protected roost to joeys, offering warm guideline, and partaking in versatile supporting during scavenging endeavors. The fair way to deal with nurturing, where the two moms and fathers add to the prosperity of posterity, challenges conventional orientation jobs inside marsupial families.

Drawing matches with human nurturing, contemporary social orders progressively perceive the significance of divided liabilities among moms and fathers. The advancement towards more evenhanded nurturing jobs among people repeats the agreeable elements saw in kangaroo families, stressing the advantages of cooperative providing care.

Transformations to Pouchless Nurturing: The Human Story

While kangaroos have advanced with particular pockets, people have adjusted to pouchless nurturing. The shortfall of an actual pocket requires elective providing care techniques, like the utilization of child transporters, carriages, and lodgings. Human newborn children, unequipped for free portability, depend on outer help designs to guarantee their security and prosperity.

Perceptions of kangaroo fathers involving their tails as steady apparatuses rouse reflection on the adaptability of human nurturing devices. From the ergonomic plan of child transporters to the essential arrangement of bunks for ideal wellbeing, human guardians, similar to kangaroo guardians, utilize versatile advancements to improve the providing care insight.

Parental Holding: Close to home Underpinnings of Being a parent

Connection Elements: Pocket Holding versus Skin-to-Skin Contact

In the kangaroo world, the pocket fills in as the focal point of connection and holding among moms and joeys. The close space takes into consideration skin-to-skin contact, establishing a tactile rich climate essential for the profound improvement of posterity.

Kangaroo moms give a warm and sustaining shelter inside the pocket, cultivating serious areas of strength for a that establishes the groundwork for the joey's personal prosperity.

In the human setting, the idea of skin-to-skin contact is stressed through practices, for example, kangaroo care for untimely babies. The purposeful and close actual contact among parental figures and babies advances profound holding, directs physiological capabilities, and adds to the general wellbeing and improvement of human infants.

Parental Presence and Solace: Cross-Species Bits of knowledge

The meaning of parental presence and solace stretches out across species limits. In kangaroo families, the pocket addresses a safe-haven where joeys track down comfort and security. The nearness of guardians, whether as a pocket or direct actual contact, fills in as a wellspring of solace for posterity during weak stages.

Human nurturing methods of reasoning stress the significance of establishing a safe and sincerely strong climate for kids. Whether through actual closeness, verbal consolation, or the arrangement of encouraging items, human guardians endeavor to lay out a feeling that everything is good and connection, reflecting the profound establishments saw in kangaroo families.

Formative Stages: From Infants to Autonomy
Infant Care: Fitting Help to Weak Posterity

Noticing kangaroo fathers adjusting their tails to support and support infant joeys gives a striking lined up with the particular consideration expected by human newborn children. Kangaroo fathers assume an involved part in establishing a protected climate for their posterity during the basic period of infant care. The tail turns into a flexible instrument, displaying the versatility of marsupial nurturing to the interesting requirements of weak babies.

In the human setting, guardians participate in closely resembling works on, using wrapping up procedures, child covers, and strong gadgets to guarantee the security and solace of babies. The fitted way to deal with infant care features the all inclusive requirement for versatile systems that address the particular prerequisites of babies during their underlying progressive phases.

Rummaging and Investigation: Portable Nurturers in Kangaroo Families

As joeys change to additional portable transformative phases, kangaroo fathers become versatile nurturers, conveying their young during scavenging endeavors. The tail, when a support, changes into a strong device that empowers fathers to give a solid roost to joeys as they investigate their environmental factors. The involved way to deal with nurturing during scavenging exercises adds to the general turn of events and schooling of youthful kangaroos.

Human guardians, as well, assume the part of versatile nurturers, working with investigation and growth opportunities for their youngsters. Whether through carriage strolls, directed trips, or regulated play, the equal elements feature the significance of parental direction and backing as posterity adventure into the more extensive world.

Instructing Minutes: Kangaroo Fathers and Human Tutors

Perceptions of kangaroo fathers filling in as coaches to their posterity during the progress to autonomy draw charming equals with human educating minutes. As joeys master fundamental abilities for endurance, fathers guide and support investigation.

The tail, when a strong device, turns into an instrument of direction, underlining the job of kangaroo fathers as guides in the formative excursion of their young.

Human guardians additionally embrace the job of coaches, giving direction, consolation, and showing minutes as their youngsters explore the way to autonomy. The common obligation to encouraging the advancement of versatile ways of behaving and abilities to survive highlights the all inclusive parts of mentorship inside the domain of nurturing.

Difficulties and Variations: Exploring Being a parent's Perplexing Landscape
Predation Dangers: Shared Worries Across Species

The difficulties of predation gambles face both kangaroo guardians and human parental figures. Perceptions of kangaroo fathers exploring the sensitive harmony between safeguarding their posterity and relieving predation chances mirror the common worries and obligations related with life as a parent in nature.

In human social orders, guardians embrace different methodologies to relieve gambles, from childproofing homes to carrying out wellbeing estimates in open air conditions. The instinctual drive to safeguard posterity from potential perils highlights the comprehensiveness of the difficulties looked by guardians across species.

Asset Shortage: Systems for Provisioning

Asset shortage presents difficulties for kangaroo fathers liable for giving food to their families. The essential changes in rummaging designs, investigation of new regions, and variation to ecological vacillations feature the flexibility and versatility expected to explore asset challenges in nature.

Also, human guardians battle with asset shortage and financial requirements as they endeavor to accommodate their families. From changing food spending plans to investigating elective assets, the equals highlight the imaginative critical thinking abilities showed by guardians notwithstanding asset challenges.

Transformative Ramifications: Life as a parent as a Versatile Benefit
Comprehensive Wellness: Amplifying Conceptive Achievement

The idea of comprehensive wellness, which thinks about the conceptive outcome of people and their family members, tracks down reverberation in both kangaroo and human nurturing procedures. Kangaroo fathers and human parental figures add to the comprehensive wellness of their particular populaces by effectively partaking in the childhood and assurance of posterity.

The arrangement with comprehensive wellness hypothesis stresses the developmental benefits presented by cooperative nurturing endeavors. The common hereditary material and helpful elements inside nuclear families add to the spread and endurance of family, intensifying the by and large regenerative progress of both kangaroo and human populaces.

Transformations to Ecological Elements

Kangaroo nurturing and human life as a parent feature versatile reactions to explicit natural elements. The fitting of nurturing techniques to suit biological specialties, asset accessibility, and predation pressures mirrors the versatile idea of nurturing ways of behaving across species.

Perceptions of kangaroo fathers flourishing in parched conditions and human guardians adjusting to assorted scenes feature the interconnectedness between nurturing procedures and natural elements. The capacity to explore and adjust to natural difficulties adds to the versatility and supportability of both kangaroo and human populaces.

5.1 Parallels between Kangaroo and Human Parenting

Nurturing, a crucial part of the animals of the world collectively, rises above species limits, featuring the common impulses and ways of behaving that support the consideration and childhood of posterity. While the distinctions among marsupials and warm blooded creatures like people are obvious, fascinating equals exist in the supporting elements of kangaroos and people. This investigation looks to unwind the consistent ideas woven into the embroidery of kangaroo and human nurturing, revealing insight into the general subjects of care, insurance, and the unpredictable bonds that structure among guardians and their young.

Kangaroo Pocket and Human Belly: Safe-havens of Development

In the two kangaroos and people, the underlying phases of posterity improvement happen in safeguarded conditions. For kangaroos, the pocket fills in as a solid sanctuary where small, immature joeys proceed with their development outside the belly. Likewise, the human belly gives a sustaining space to fetal turn of events, offering security and food until the hour of birth.

While the physical designs vary, the idea of a devoted space for early improvement reverberates across species. Both the kangaroo pocket and the human belly represent the asylums where the underpinnings of life are laid, featuring the instinctual drive to make ideal circumstances for posterity development.

Maternal Presence and Holding

Maternal holding is a foundation of both kangaroo and human nurturing. In kangaroos, this bond is fashioned through closeness and the steady presence of the joey in the pocket. The mother gives warmth, sustenance, and a conviction that all is good, cultivating a profound close to home association with her posterity.

In human nurturing, the holding system starts in the belly, where the creating embryo encounters the musical pulsating of the mother's heart and offers in her physiological encounters. After birth, the close bond reinforces through actual contact, breastfeeding, and the arrangement of solace and consolation. The quintessence of maternal presence, portrayed by profound attunement and responsiveness to the requirements of the posterity, rises above species limits.

Sustaining through Milk: The Consistent idea of Lactation

One of the most basic equals among kangaroo and human nurturing lies in the arrangement of sustenance through milk. Both kangaroo moms and human moms produce milk explicitly custom fitted to the requirements of their young. The sythesis of marsupial milk, however exceptional in its attributes, fills a similar need as human bosom milk - to give fundamental supplements, antibodies, and development factors urgent for the improvement of the posterity.

The demonstration of breastfeeding, whether it's the kangaroo joey hooking onto its mom's nipple inside the pocket or the human baby nursing at the bosom, highlights the private association laid out through the trading of sustenance. Past the healthful perspective, breastfeeding cultivates close to home holding, solace, and a feeling that everything is good, epitomizing the general subject of maternal consideration.

Parental Penance and Versatile Procedures

Both kangaroo and human guardians show momentous versatile methodologies and a readiness to make penances for the prosperity of their posterity. In kangaroos, maternal penance is clear in the one of a kind conceptive cycle. Female kangaroos put vigorously in development, birth, and lactation, bearing the obligation of giving ideal circumstances to their young regardless of the difficulties of the Australian climate.

Human guardians, as well, experience a horde of penances, from the actual cost of pregnancy and labor to the continuous obligation to addressing the requirements of their kids.

The eagerness to put the requirements of posterity first, frequently at individual expense, mirrors a common instinctual drive towards guaranteeing the endurance and progress of the future.

Educating and Learning: Formative Achievements

The most common way of instructing and learning is a central part of both kangaroo and human nurturing. In kangaroos, joeys go through a time of pocket reliance where they master fundamental abilities for endurance. The mother gives information through directed investigation, play, and perception, step by step permitting the joey to foster freedom.

Additionally, human guardians guide their kids through formative achievements. From the initial steps to the obtaining of language and interactive abilities, guardians assume a critical part in working with opportunities for growth. The equal falsehoods in the demonstration of educating as well as in the steady change from reliance to freedom, denoting a common excursion of development and improvement.

Security and Sanctuary: Making Places of refuge

Safeguarding posterity and giving sanctuary is a common topic in both kangaroo and human nurturing. For kangaroos, the pocket fills in as a versatile place of refuge, protecting joeys from hunters and natural risks. As the joey develops, the pocket changes into a space where the youthful marsupial can look for shelter when required.

In human nurturing, the idea of making places of refuge appears in different structures - from the actual sanctuary of a home to the profound wellbeing given by parental direction and backing. Both kangaroo moms and human guardians share the nature to safeguard their young from hurt, establishing conditions helpful for development and security.

Social Elements: Nuclear families and Emotionally supportive networks

The significance of social elements and the development of nuclear families is obvious in both kangaroo and human social orders. Kangaroo moms frequently raise their joeys in affectionate gatherings, giving open doors to social collaboration and learning. Essentially, human families structure the basic social unit where youngsters learn normal practices, values, and relational abilities.

Both kangaroo and human posterity benefit from the emotionally supportive networks laid out inside their separate social designs. Whether it's the cooperative endeavors of kangaroo moms in collective consideration or the multi-generational encouraging groups of people in human families, the meaning of social bonds and agreeable nurturing rises above species qualifications.

Variations to Natural Difficulties

Kangaroo and human nurturing exhibit surprising variations to ecological difficulties. Kangaroos, local to the different scenes of Australia, have developed techniques to flourish in factor and once in a while unforgiving circumstances. The capacity to change regenerative rates in light of ecological elements is an outstanding transformation, permitting kangaroos to upgrade the possibilities posterity endurance in view of asset accessibility.

Human guardians, as well, explore ecological difficulties, but in various settings. Whether it's adjusting to financial circumstances, social impacts, or changes in the worldwide scene, human guardians show strength and adaptability in accommodating their kids' requirements. The common ability to adjust to ecological difficulties exhibits the flexibility inborn in nurturing senses.

5.2 Lessons We Can Learn from Kangaroo Parenting

Nurturing is a complicated and significant excursion, and nature furnishes us with different models of providing care techniques. Kangaroos, the notable marsupials of Australia, offer special experiences into nurturing that reach out past their unmistakable science. In this investigation, we disentangle the examples we can gain from kangaroo nurturing, drawing motivation from their versatile ways of behaving, strength, and the complicated elements of marsupial day to day life.

1. **Flexibility in Nurturing Systems**

   Kangaroo nurturing shows us the significance of flexibility in nurturing systems. Not at all like vertebrates with a placental conceptive framework, kangaroos have advanced a particular strategy where their young are conceived rashly and proceed with their improvement in the wellbeing of the pocket. This versatile methodology permits kangaroos to flourish in different and frequently testing conditions.

   The illustration here is to perceive the requirement for adaptability in our nurturing approaches. Every kid is special, and conditions can differ. Being available to adjusting our procedures in light of the singular requirements and difficulties introduced by our kids considers a more responsive and compelling nurturing venture.

2. **Significance of Actual Contact**

   Actual contact is a crucial part of kangaroo nurturing and an example that reverberates profoundly with human guardians. Kangaroo moms, using their pockets, give a steady and secure space for their joeys. This actual closeness offers warmth and insurance as well as cultivates major areas of strength for a bond.

   In the buzzing about of current life, where computerized screens and virtual correspondence frequently outweigh everything else, the illustration from kangaroos is to focus on and esteem actual touch.

   From holding our babies to embracing our more established youngsters, actual contact is a strong method for correspondence and association that adds to a kid's personal prosperity.

3. **Shared Parental Obligations**

   Kangaroo nurturing frequently includes shared parental obligations. While the mother gives the pocket to security and sustenance, the dad assumes a functioning part in providing care, particularly as the joey develops and turns out to be more versatile. This common way to deal with nurturing accentuates the significance of the two guardians in the childhood of posterity.

   In human families, the illustration is to perceive and value the commitments of the two guardians. Shared liabilities make a more adjusted and steady family climate. From diaper changes to sleep time stories, including the two guardians in different parts of providing care advances the nurturing experience and fortifies family bonds.

4. **Sustaining Autonomy Step by step**

   As kangaroo joeys develop, they change from the pocket to additional autonomous progressive phases. Kangaroo nurturing shows us the craft of sustaining autonomy slowly. The mother supports investigation and getting the hang of, permitting the joey to foster fundamental basic instincts while giving a well-being net when required.

   In human nurturing, this example underlines the significance of cultivating autonomy in our kids. Permitting them to take age-proper dangers, simply decide, and gain from encounters fabricates certainty and versatility. Perceiving when to offer help and when to energize freedom is a fragile equilibrium that adds to a kid's sound turn of events.

5. **Custom fitted Nurturing Approaches**

   Kangaroo nurturing features the meaning of custom fitted nurturing approaches. With the shortfall of a conventional pocket in male kangaroos, they have adjusted by utilizing areas of strength for them to make a solid roost for their joeys. This tail-as-pocket procedure features the flexibility of nurturing approaches in view of the special requirements of the posterity.

Human guardians can gain from this illustration by perceiving that there is nobody size-fits-all way to deal with nurturing. Every youngster is a person with particular qualities, difficulties, and inclinations. Fitting our nurturing styles to meet the particular requirements of every youngster takes into consideration a more viable and responsive providing care insight.

6. **Flexibility Notwithstanding Difficulties**

Kangaroo nurturing unfurls in the difficult scenes of Australia, where asset accessibility can be flighty, and ecological circumstances are unforgiving. Regardless of these difficulties, kangaroo moms show strength in accommodating their young. They change conceptive rates in view of ecological variables, exhibiting versatility and perseverance.

The example for human guardians is to embrace flexibility despite life's difficulties. Nurturing accompanies its portion of vulnerabilities and hardships, and the capacity to adjust and persevere chasing the prosperity of our youngsters is a significant quality. Strength permits us to explore the high points and low points of nurturing with a positive outlook and a pledge to development.

7. **Ecological Mindfulness and Protection**

Kangaroo nurturing likewise offers an illustration in ecological mindfulness and protection. The endurance of kangaroo families is complicatedly associated with the soundness of their normal environments. Protection endeavors that focus on natural surroundings conservation and reclamation add to the prosperity of kangaroos and their posterity.

For human guardians, this example underlines the significance of imparting natural mindfulness and a feeling of obligation for protection in our kids. Helping them to appreciate and safeguard the normal world makes an establishment for people in the future focused on natural stewardship.

8. **Holding Through Play and Investigation**

Kangaroo joeys take part in energetic exercises and investigation as a component of their turn of events. Kangaroo nurturing shows us the significance of holding through play and shared encounters. Lively collaborations add to the close to home association between kangaroo moms and joeys and give significant learning valuable open doors.

In human families, the illustration is to focus on play as a fundamental component of holding. Whether it's innovative play, open air exercises, or inventive pursuits, shared snapshots of delight and investigation fortify the parent-kid bond. Perky connections likewise add to a youngster's mental, personal, and social turn of events.

9. **Acknowledgment of the Implicit Commitments**

Kangaroo nurturing, particularly the job of male kangaroos, features the implicit commitments frequently ignored in conventional nurturing accounts. While female kangaroos are commended for their pocket nurturing, the dynamic inclusion of male kangaroos challenges generalizations and highlights the variety of nurturing jobs.

In human nurturing, the illustration is to perceive and value the implicit commitments, everything being equal. Whether it's dads, grandparents, or other strong figures, recognizing the shifted manners by which people add to the prosperity of youngsters encourages a culture of appreciation and inclusivity inside the family.

10. **Constant Learning and Variation**

Kangaroo nurturing is a dynamic and developing interaction. As joeys develop and natural circumstances change, kangaroo guardians persistently adjust their nurturing procedures. This illustration highlights the significance of constant learning and transformation in the nurturing venture.

For human guardians, the example is to approach nurturing as an excursion of development and revelation. Staying open to gaining from encounters, looking for new information, and adjusting our methodologies in view of developing conditions add to a really enhancing and satisfying nurturing experience.

5.3 Practical Applications for Modern Families

As families explore the intricacies of current life, the insight got from nature's providing care models, for example, kangaroo nurturing, can be applied to address the difficulties and upgrade the delights of contemporary family living. In this investigation, we dive into functional applications propelled by kangaroo nurturing, offering bits of knowledge and systems that advanced families can coordinate into their regular routines. From encouraging versatility to focusing on association, these commonsense applications give a guide to supporting strong, amicable, and satisfying relational intricacies.

1. **Focusing on Actual Association in the Computerized Age**
   In a world overwhelmed by screens and virtual correspondence, the significance of actual association couldn't possibly be more significant. Enlivened by kangaroo nurturing, where actual contact is a foundation of providing care, current families can focus on material cooperations to fortify bonds. Straightforward motions like embraces, snuggles, and actual play make an unmistakable feeling of association, cultivating profound prosperity for the two guardians and youngsters.
   Useful Application: Lay out an everyday schedule that incorporates deliberate snapshots of actual association. Whether it's a morning embrace, a night nestle, or a family dance meeting, these minutes add to a positive and sustaining family climate.

2. **Fitting Nurturing Ways to deal with Individual Requirements**
   Kangaroo nurturing underlines the significance of custom fitted ways to deal

with providing care in light of individual necessities. Current families can profit from embracing a customized nurturing reasoning that perceives and answers the interesting qualities, qualities, and difficulties of every relative. Understanding that there is nobody size-fits-all approach considers adaptability and flexibility in exploring the assorted scene of everyday life.

Down to earth Application: Participate in open correspondence inside the family to see every part's inclinations, awarenesses, and learning styles. Tailor nurturing systems to oblige individual requirements, establishing a climate where everybody feels seen, heard, and upheld.

3. **Making Places of refuge for Open Correspondence**

The idea of making places of refuge for investigation and learning, as seen in kangaroo nurturing, is appropriate to cultivating open correspondence inside current families. Laying out a climate where relatives feel open to offering viewpoints, feelings, and concerns adds to solid connections and a conviction that all is good.

Useful Application: Assign explicit times or spaces for family conversations where everybody has a potential chance to share their contemplations without judgment. Empower undivided attention and approval of sentiments, encouraging a culture of open correspondence that reinforces family bonds.

4. **Sustaining Autonomy Slowly**

Kangaroo nurturing shows us the craft of supporting freedom progressively, permitting posterity to investigate and learn while giving a security net when required. Present day families can apply this example by encouraging age-suitable freedom in youngsters. Empowering liability, navigation, and critical thinking abilities adds to the improvement of certain and independent people.

Viable Application: Include kids in dynamic cycles at home, permitting them to add to family decisions. Give chances to progress in years fitting liabilities, step by step expanding independence as youngsters show status. This approach develops a feeling of freedom and obligation.

5. **Offsetting Screen Time with Outside Investigation**

As families wrestle with the ubiquity of screens, the illustration from kangaroo nurturing about the significance of play and investigation can direct present day families in tracking down an equilibrium.

Incorporating open air exercises into day to day schedules advances actual wellbeing, mental turn of events, and significant family associations.

Useful Application: Assign explicit times for open air exercises, whether it's a family nature walk, cultivating together, or participating in outside games. Making without tech zones during specific hours energizes dynamic play, encouraging a good arrangement between screen time and certifiable encounters.

6. **Shared Liabilities and Emotionally supportive networks**

The accentuation on shared parental obligations in kangaroo nurturing features the meaning of an emotionally supportive network inside the family. Current families can profit from perceiving and valuing the different commitments of all relatives, cultivating a cooperative and steady environment.

Down to earth Application: Lay out a family schedule that includes shared liabilities, permitting every part to add to day to day undertakings. Perceive and offer thanks for the interesting commitments of relatives, making a feeling of cooperation and shared help.

7. **Empowering Constant Learning and Variation**

Kangaroo nurturing flourishes with constant learning and transformation to evolving conditions. This example is appropriate to present day families confronting the unique scene of contemporary life. The capacity to adjust, gain from encounters, and develop all together fortifies flexibility and cohesiveness.

Useful Application: Develop a mentality of nonstop advancing inside the family. Energize interest, investigation, and a readiness to attempt new things together. Embrace difficulties as any open doors for development, cultivating a culture of versatility and shared learning.

8. **Perceiving and Observing Implicit Commitments**

The example of perceiving and celebrating implicit commitments from kangaroo nurturing difficulties customary stories and highlights the significance of recognizing all guardians inside the family. Present day families can profit from esteeming and offering thanks for the bunch ways people add to the family's prosperity.

Down to earth Application: Carry out normal family appreciation minutes where every part shares their appreciation for the commitments of others. Recognize the implicit endeavors that frequently slip by everyone's notice, making a culture of appreciation and confirmation inside the family.

9. **Ingraining Natural Mindfulness and Obligation**

The association between kangaroo nurturing and natural mindfulness recommends a more extensive example about obligation towards the world we occupy. Current families can draw motivation from this example by imparting a feeling of natural cognizance and obligation in their kids.

Down to earth Application: Take part in eco-accommodating practices as a family, like reusing, decreasing waste, and taking part in protection drives. Teach youngsters about the significance of ecological stewardship, encouraging a feeling of obligation for the planet they acquire.

10. **Embracing Strength in Everyday Life**

The strength showed by kangaroo guardians in testing conditions offers a significant example for present day families confronting their own arrangement of difficulties. Embracing versatility as a family advances a positive mentality, flexibility, and the capacity to explore misfortune together.

Functional Application: Cultivate strength through open correspondence about challenges and the significance of supporting each other during troublesome times. Develop a family climate where difficulties are seen as any open doors for learning and development, reinforcing the family's aggregate strength.

Chapter 6

Challenges and Solutions

In the consistently developing scene of our worldwide society, challenges arise as regular results of progress and change. From mechanical progressions to social and natural moves, our reality is continually confronted with obstacles that request consideration and inventive arrangements. This exposition investigates different difficulties across various spaces, giving a top to bottom examination of the snags we experience in our contemporary presence.

1. **Mechanical Difficulties**
1. **Online protection Dangers**

    In a time overwhelmed by innovation, one of the preeminent difficulties is the raising danger of online protection breaks. With the rising interconnectedness of gadgets and organizations, people and associations the same are helpless against assaults that can think twice about data, prompting monetary misfortunes and security breaks.
2. **Fast Mechanical Progressions**

While mechanical advancement brings various advantages, the fast speed of development additionally presents difficulties. The tenacious quest for state of the art arrangements frequently dominates administrative systems and moral contemplations, making a situation where society battles to stay aware of the ramifications of new innovations like man-made reasoning, biotechnology, and quantum processing.

II. Ecological Difficulties

1. **Environmental Change**

    Maybe the most squeezing challenge within recent memory, environmental change represents a danger to the actual texture of our planet. Increasing temperatures, outrageous climate occasions, and the exhaustion of regular assets are ramifications of human exercises that request pressing and composed world-wide activity.

2. Contamination

Different types of contamination, including air, water, and soil contamination, add to ecological debasement. Modern exercises, ill-advised garbage removal, and over-consumption have brought about biological systems under serious pressure, affecting biodiversity and human wellbeing.

III. Social Difficulties

1. Monetary Disparity

The developing hole between the rich and the unfortunate presents a critical social test. Monetary imbalance can prompt social agitation, hamper instructive open doors, and impede generally speaking cultural advancement. Resolving this issue requires a thorough methodology including strategy changes, instruction changes, and social drives.

2. Separation and Bad form

Regardless of progress in advancing correspondence, separation and treachery persevere in different structures, including racial, orientation, and financial differences. Defeating these difficulties requires cultural thoughtfulness, training, and the execution of approaches that advance inclusivity and decency.

IV. Medical services Difficulties

1. Worldwide Pandemics

The episode of worldwide pandemics, as seen with the Coronavirus pandemic, features the weaknesses of our medical services frameworks. The fast spread of irresistible illnesses can overpower medical care foundation, requiring worked on worldwide participation, readiness, and medical care advancement.

2. Admittance to Medical care

Differences in medical care access endure universally, with millions coming up short on fundamental clinical benefits. Tending to this challenge requires extending medical care framework as well as addressing financial variables that add to inconsistent access.

V. Political Difficulties

1. International Strains

In an interconnected world, international strains between countries present difficulties to worldwide strength. Issues like regional questions, asset contest, and philosophical contrasts can prompt contentions that influence a great many lives.

2. Administration and Defilement

Powerful administration is essential for cultural prosperity, however defilement stays a huge deterrent. Defilement disintegrates trust in establishments, hampers monetary turn of events, and sustains disparity, requiring changes in administration structures and expanded straightforwardness.

VI. Instructive Difficulties

1. **Admittance to Quality Schooling**
   While instruction is in many cases considered a pathway to advance, millions all over the planet need admittance to quality training. Monetary inconsistencies, orientation inclination, and insufficient framework add to instructive disparity, blocking the advancement of people and social orders.

2. **Mechanical Disturbance in Schooling**

The reconciliation of innovation in schooling, while at the same time promising, additionally presents difficulties. The computerized partition, worries about information protection, and the requirement for compelling instructor preparing are issues that should be addressed to guarantee that mechanical progressions upgrade as opposed to ruin instructive results.

6.1 Environmental Threats to Kangaroo Parenting

Kangaroo nurturing, enlivened by the marsupial consideration model, has acquired notoriety as a supporting way to deal with newborn child care. This training includes delayed skin-to-skin contact between the guardian and the baby, working with profound holding and ideal turn of events. Nonetheless, the adequacy of kangaroo nurturing isn't resistant to natural dangers. This exposition dives into the different natural difficulties that posture dangers to kangaroo nurturing, investigating how factors, for example, environmental change, contamination, and urbanization influence this nurturing strategy.

1. **The Substance of Kangaroo Nurturing**
1. **Verifiable Setting**
   Kangaroo nurturing, otherwise called kangaroo care or skin-to-healthy skin, draws motivation from the kangaroo's normal technique for really focusing on its young. The idea began in neonatal consideration, essentially in light of the requirement for elective techniques for really focusing on untimely newborn children. It includes setting the baby in direct skin contact with the guardian, normally the parent, establishing a supporting climate that advances physical and close to home prosperity.

2. Advantages of Kangaroo Nurturing

The act of kangaroo nurturing has been related with a bunch of advantages for the two babies and guardians. These incorporate superior holding, improved mental and close to home turn of events, better rest designs, and a decreased gamble of different medical problems for the newborn child. Kangaroo nurturing has likewise been found to decidedly affect breastfeeding and maternal psychological well-being.

II. Environmental Change and Kangaroo Nurturing

1. Temperature Limits

One of the principal parts of kangaroo nurturing is keeping a steady and agreeable temperature for the baby. Environmental change, nonetheless, is prompting more regular and serious temperature limits, which can present difficulties for keeping up with the ideal circumstances expected for kangaroo care. Climbing temperatures might bring about inconvenience for both the parent and the newborn child, influencing the viability of skin-to-skin contact.

2. Influence on Untimely Newborn children

Untimely newborn children, who are especially powerless, may confront expanded gambles because of the ecological changes related with environmental change. Outrageous intensity occasions can compound existing wellbeing concerns, and the potential for additional incessant and serious climate occasions might upset medical services administrations, influencing the accessibility of offices prepared for kangaroo care.

III. Contamination and Kangaroo Nurturing

1. Air Contamination

Urbanization and industrialization add to raised degrees of air contamination, which can inconveniently affect babies going through kangaroo care. Unfortunate air quality can worsen respiratory issues, influencing the respiratory improvement of untimely newborn children. Also, openness to poisons might present dangers to the strength of both the parent and the newborn child during stretched out times of skin-to-skin contact.

2. Ecological Poisons

The presence of ecological poisons, like pesticides and weighty metals, can unfavorably affect the soundness of babies. As kangaroo nurturing includes direct skin contact, there is a gamble of poison move from the parental figure to the baby. Tending to contamination is, in this way, essential to guaranteeing a protected climate for powerful kangaroo care.

IV. Urbanization and Kangaroo Nurturing

1. **Restricted Green Spaces**

   Urbanization frequently prompts the decrease of green spaces and indigenous habitats. The absence of admittance to green regions might restrict valuable open doors for guardians to participate in kangaroo care outside, reducing the potential advantages related with openness to nature. Also, the substantial wilderness might add to raised feelings of anxiety for guardians, influencing the nature of skin-to-skin contact.

2. **Commotion and Light Contamination**

   Metropolitan conditions are described by elevated degrees of commotion and light contamination, which can upset the rest designs critical for newborn child advancement. Kangaroo nurturing, especially during the early months, requires a quiet and calm climate. The consistent openness to metropolitan clamor and light might thwart the adequacy of this nurturing approach, possibly influencing both the parent and the baby.

V. Financial Variables and Kangaroo Nurturing

1. **Openness to Assets**

   Financial elements assume a critical part in deciding the openness of assets important for powerful kangaroo nurturing. Admittance to medical care offices, instructive materials, and encouraging groups of people can be restricted in financially distraught networks. This absence of assets might thwart guardians from taking on and supporting kangaroo care rehearses.

2. **Parental Pressure and Kangaroo Nurturing**

   Financial difficulties, including monetary pressure and restricted social help, can add to parental pressure. Stress has been connected to less viable kangaroo nurturing, possibly decreasing the positive results related with this providing care technique. Tending to financial abberations is fundamental for advancing broad reception of kangaroo care.

VI. Creative Arrangements and Future Contemplations

1. **Mechanical Developments**

   Progressions in innovation offer likely answers for a portion of the ecological dangers to kangaroo nurturing. For instance, wearable gadgets with environment control elements can assist with managing the temperature for both the parent and the baby during skin-to-skin contact. Furthermore, telehealth administrations can offer help and direction for guardians rehearsing kangaroo care, spanning holes in medical services openness.

2. **Reasonable Metropolitan Preparation**

   Taking into account the effect of urbanization on kangaroo nurturing, reasonable metropolitan arranging becomes essential. Planning urban areas with more than adequate green spaces, lessening clamor and light contamination, and advancing local area prosperity can establish conditions helpful for viable kangaroo care. This requires coordinated effort between metropolitan organizers, policymakers, and medical services experts.

3. **Public Mindfulness and Instruction**

Bringing issues to light about the ecological dangers to kangaroo nurturing and advancing training on supportable practices can enable guardians to go with informed decisions. Instructive missions can resolve issues, for example, environmental change, contamination, and the significance of green spaces, cultivating a feeling of obligation toward establishing a helpful climate for kangaroo care.

6.2 Resilience and Adaptability

In the speedy and steadily changing scene of the advanced world, the capacity to explore difficulties and vulnerabilities has become progressively vital. Flexibility and versatility are two interconnected ideas that assume a significant part in people, associations, and social orders as they face and conquer different impediments. In this exposition, we will dive into the implications, significance, and reasonable utilizations of versatility and flexibility, investigating how they add to self-improvement, authoritative achievement, and cultural advancement.

Figuring out Flexibility:

Flexibility can be characterized as the ability to return from affliction, recuperate rapidly from misfortunes, and adjust emphatically despite difficulties. It goes past simple endurance and includes flourishing in the fallout of challenges. Versatile people have the psychological and profound solidarity to face mishaps, gain from them, and arise more grounded.

Clinicians frequently allude to flexibility as a powerful cycle instead of a static characteristic. This suggests that versatility can be developed and created after some time. The capacity to return from difficulty includes a blend of individual qualities, methods for dealing with stress, and natural elements.

Key Parts of Versatility:

Close to home Guideline:

Tough people are proficient at dealing with their feelings, keeping a cool head in upsetting circumstances, and really exploring a scope of sentiments. Profound guideline is essential for keeping away from the adverse impacts of persistent pressure and keeping up with mental prosperity.

Hopefulness and Positive Attitude:

An uplifting perspective on life is a sign of versatility. Hopeful people will generally see difficulties as impermanent and explicit instead of extremely durable and widely inclusive. This outlook works with a proactive way to deal with critical thinking and a faith in one's capacity to defeat difficulties.

Versatility:

Versatility, an idea firmly entwined with flexibility, includes the capacity to conform to new conditions and embrace change. Being versatile permits people to flourish in unique conditions, as they can rapidly master and apply new abilities, techniques, and points of view.

Social Help:

Solid social associations and encouraging groups of people contribute essentially to versatility. Having a dependable emotionally supportive network gives people the profound assets expected to explore testing times. Social help can emerge out of family, companions, partners, or local gatherings.

The Significance of Flexibility:

Self-awareness:

Flexibility assumes a fundamental part in self-awareness. People who develop strength frequently view difficulties as any open doors for development and self-revelation. Beating misfortune cultivates a feeling of skill and certainty, prompting expanded confidence.

Stress The executives:

The capacity to return from misfortunes is urgent for overseeing pressure really. Versatile people are less inclined to be overpowered by stressors, and they show a more prominent ability to adapt to strain, vulnerability, and unforeseen occasions.

Proficient Achievement:

In the expert domain, versatility is a critical indicator of progress. Notwithstanding quickly changing business sectors and ventures, versatile people can explore vulnerabilities, master new abilities, and position themselves as significant resources for managers.

Grasping Flexibility:

Flexibility is the ability to conform to new circumstances, changes, or difficulties. It includes being available to advancement, embracing change, and proactively looking for arrangements in unique conditions. While strength centers around the capacity to return quickly from difficulties, versatility underlines the continuous course of changing in accordance with advancing conditions.

Key Parts of Versatility:

Receptiveness:

A versatile individual is available to novel thoughts, points of view, and approaches to getting things done. This transparency encourages inventiveness and development, permitting people to investigate novel ways to deal with critical thinking.

Nonstop Learning:

Flexibility requires a promise to long lasting learning. This includes remaining informed about industry patterns, obtaining new abilities, and effectively looking for potential open doors for individual and expert turn of events.

Adaptability:

Adaptability is a foundation of versatility. Having the option to change plans and techniques because of changing conditions is fundamental for progress in powerful conditions. Unbending nature can prompt stagnation, while adaptability empowers positive progress.

Proactive Critical thinking:

Versatile people don't simply respond to transform; they proactively look for arrangements and open doors. This proactive outlook permits them to explore vulnerabilities with a feeling of organization and control.

The Interchange Among Flexibility and Versatility:

Strength and versatility are interconnected and integral ideas. While strength gives the establishment to beating mishaps and keeping up with prosperity despite misfortune, versatility prepares people to flourish in a consistently impacting world. Together, they structure a unique arrangement of abilities that enable people to really explore difficulties and vulnerabilities.

Strength as an Establishment:

Flexibility fills in as an establishment for versatility. At the point when people have the capacity to return from difficulties, they are bound to move toward really impact with a positive outlook. Flexibility gives the profound and mental strength expected to face the vulnerabilities related with adjusting to new conditions.

Versatility as an Impetus:

Then again, versatility catalyzes flexibility by empowering people to proactively embrace change. The ability to acclimate to new circumstances and look for imaginative arrangements improves a singular's capacity to effectively explore difficulties. Flexibility enhances the viability of versatility in a quickly developing world.

Input Circle:

Versatility and flexibility structure a criticism circle, where the improvement of one supports the other. The experience of beating difficulties and adjusting to change adds to the development of strength. Thus, a strong outlook works with a more versatile way to deal with future vulnerabilities.

Useful Utilizations of Flexibility and Versatility:

In the Working environment:

In the present powerful business climate, strength and versatility are profoundly esteemed characteristics. Representatives who can return from mishaps and promptly adjust to changes contribute altogether to the outcome of associations. Businesses progressively perceive the significance of encouraging a strong and versatile labor force through preparing programs and steady workplaces.

Training and Learning:

The schooling area plays a basic part in developing strength and flexibility in understudies. By advancing a development mentality, empowering critical thinking abilities, and establishing a steady learning climate, teachers can outfit understudies with the devices expected to flourish in a consistently impacting world.

Self-awareness:

People can effectively develop flexibility and versatility through different self-improvement procedures. This might incorporate rehearsing care and stress-the board procedures, looking for different learning potential open doors, and building solid social associations. Participating in nonstop self-reflection likewise improves the ability to gain from encounters and foster a strong outlook.

Local area and Cultural Strength:

Strength and versatility are not restricted to people; they are likewise fundamental for the flexibility of networks and social orders. Despite difficulties like cataclysmic events, monetary changes, or worldwide wellbeing emergencies, networks that are tough and versatile can recuperate all the more rapidly and fabricate a manageable future.

Difficulties to Flexibility and Versatility:

Feeling of dread toward Disappointment:

The apprehension about disappointment can thwart both flexibility and versatility. People who fear committing errors might battle to return from difficulties, and the apprehension about disappointment can likewise prompt obstruction against change. Defeating this dread includes cultivating a culture that embraces disappointment as a learning a potential open door and perceives the worth of flexibility even with difficulties.

Absence of Emotionally supportive networks:

An absence of social help can subvert versatility. People confronting difficulties without a solid emotionally supportive network might find it more challenging to quickly return from difficulty. Building solid social associations and encouraging groups of people is fundamental for cultivating strength.

Protection from Change:

Protection from change is a typical boundary to flexibility. A few people and associations oppose groundbreaking thoughts and approaches to getting things done because of a feeling of dread toward the obscure or a craving to keep up with the norm. Defeating protection from change includes cultivating a culture that values development and persistent improvement.

Burnout:

Unreasonable pressure and responsibility can prompt burnout, adversely influencing both flexibility and versatility. Burnout lessens a singular's ability to return from difficulties and hampers their capacity to adjust to new difficulties. Carrying out systems for stress the executives and balance between fun and serious activities is urgent for relieving the gamble of burnout.

6.3 Comparisons with Human Parenting Challenges

Nurturing is a widespread and immortal undertaking, forming the texture of social orders across societies and ages. While the encounters of nurturing are divided between people, different species in the animals of the world collectively likewise display extraordinary nurturing difficulties. In this paper, we will dig into a similar investigation of human nurturing difficulties, drawing equals and differentiations with nurturing difficulties saw in the animals of the world collectively. By looking at the likenesses and contrasts, we expect to acquire experiences into the different procedures utilized by guardians across species and the consistent ideas that tight spot the intricacies of nurturing.

Human Nurturing Difficulties:
Mental Turn of events:

Human newborn children are brought into the world with an exceptional level of mental youthfulness contrasted with numerous different species. The drawn out time of reliance and the fast mental improvement during youth present interesting difficulties for human guardians. The requirement for consistent consideration, excitement, and direction to help mental development can interest.

Training and Socialization:

Human guardians face the test of not just accommodating the actual requirements of their youngsters yet in addition guaranteeing their schooling and socialization. The transmission of social qualities, normal practices, and moral standards turns into a critical obligation regarding guardians as they guide their youngsters toward becoming contributing citizenry.

Close to home and Mental Turn of events:

The many-sided close to home and mental improvement of human kids adds layers of intricacy to nurturing. Supporting ability to understand people at their core, overseeing pressure and uneasiness, and cultivating versatility are essential parts of human nurturing difficulties. Guardians assume a significant part in giving a protected profound establishment to their kids to explore the intricacies of the human experience.

Adjusting Work and Family:

In the cutting edge world, guardians frequently wrestle with the test of offsetting work liabilities with family commitments. Shuffling profession goals with the requests of nurturing demands viable using time effectively, correspondence, and emotionally supportive networks. Finding some kind of harmony is difficult for the overwhelming majority contemporary guardians.

Innovation and Screen Time:

The coming of innovation has presented another arrangement of difficulties for guardians. Overseeing screen time, exploring the computerized scene, and guaranteeing a sound connection with innovation are worries that past ages didn't confront. Human guardians should remain educated about the potential effect regarding innovation on youngster advancement and arrive at informed conclusions about its utilization.

Creature Nurturing Difficulties: A Near Point of view:
Instinctual versus Learned Ways of behaving:

Dissimilar to people, numerous creature species depend basically on instinctual ways of behaving for nurturing. While certain species display noteworthy parental impulses, others might have to master nurturing ways of behaving through perception and experience. The harmony between inborn ways of behaving and learned reactions differs across species.

Step by step processes for surviving:

Creature guardians face the consistent test of guaranteeing the endurance of their posterity in nature. This might include showing abilities to survive, giving assurance from hunters, and getting food sources. The endurance challenges are frequently prompt and perilous, requiring speedy and instinctual reactions.

Restricted Correspondence:

Correspondence among parent and posterity in the collective of animals is much of the time restricted contrasted with the unpredictable language and relational abilities of people. Creature guardians should depend on non-verbal prompts, non-verbal communication, and vocalizations to pass significant data on to their young. The productivity of correspondence is urgent for the endurance of the species.

Maternal Speculation:

Numerous creature species show fluctuating levels of maternal venture, for certain moms giving broad consideration and assurance to their posterity, while others might have more restricted contribution. The level of maternal speculation is frequently affected by elements like the species' conceptive methodology, ecological circumstances, and the necessities of the posterity.

Adjusting to Natural Changes:

Creature guardians should adjust rapidly to changes in their current circumstance, remembering varieties for environment, food accessibility, and living space conditions. The capacity to change nurturing systems because of natural changes is basic for the endurance of the species.

Relative Experiences and Reflections:

Parental Penance:

Both human and creature guardians show a striking limit with regards to forfeit to guarantee the prosperity of their posterity. Whether it's a human parent working extended periods to accommodate their youngster's schooling or a bird steadily chasing after food to take care of its chicks, the subject of parental penance is woven into the texture of nurturing across species.

Formative Achievements:

While the particulars of formative achievements differ, the idea of directing posterity through key phases of development is a common part of nurturing. Human guardians commend their kid's initial steps and first words, while creature guardians might praise achievements like a fruitful chase or the fledging of their young from the home.

Defensive Impulses:

Both human and creature guardians display defensive senses to safeguard their posterity from hurt. This might include actual security, showing basic instincts, or laying out regions to avert likely dangers. The inborn drive to guarantee the wellbeing of posterity is a general part of nurturing.

Gaining as a matter of fact:

Gaining as a matter of fact is a consistent theme in nurturing, rising above species limits. Human guardians draw on their own encounters and the insight went down through ages, while creature guardians depend on instinctual ways of behaving refined through transformative cycles. The interaction among intuition and learned ways of behaving is an intriguing part of nurturing across the collective of animals.

Variety in Nurturing Techniques:

The variety of nurturing techniques across species features the flexibility of nurturing to different biological specialties. From the complex consideration given by elephants to the freedom empowered in some bird species, nurturing systems mirror the extraordinary difficulties and open doors introduced by various conditions.

Chapter 7

Scientific Insights

Logical bits of knowledge structure the bedrock of how we might interpret the world, from the minuscule domains of particles to the huge territories of the universe. The quest for information through logical request has molded the course of mankind's set of experiences, prompting notable revelations that have changed our lives and extended how we might interpret the universe. In this extensive investigation, we will dive into different logical disciplines, disclosing the experiences that have characterized and keep on forming how we might interpret the normal world.

1. **Material science: Disentangling the Crucial Powers**
   The Quantum Domain:
   At the front of logical bits of knowledge lies the domain of quantum physical science, a field that investigates the way of behaving of issue and energy at the littlest scales. Quantum mechanics, with its standards of superposition and ensnarement, has altered how we might interpret particles like electrons and photons. The improvement of quantum innovations, including quantum registering and cryptography, remains as a demonstration of the groundbreaking force of bits of knowledge acquired from the quantum world.
   Relativity and the Universe:
   Albert Einstein's speculations of relativity, extraordinary and general, have given significant bits of knowledge into the idea of room, time, and gravity. From the relativistic consequences for time enlargement to the twisting of light in gravitational fields, these hypotheses have not exclusively been tentatively affirmed yet additionally act as the establishment for how we might interpret the universe on both grandiose and minute scales.

2. **Science: Divulging the Secrets of Life**
   Hereditary qualities and DNA:
   The disclosure of the design of DNA by James Watson and Francis Kink in 1953 denoted a turning point in science. Understanding the twofold helix and the

hereditary code made ready for unwinding the complexities of legacy, advancement, and the sub-atomic premise of life. The field of genomics, impelled by mechanical progressions, keeps on yielding bits of knowledge into the intricate transaction of qualities and ecological variables.

Developmental Science:

Charles Darwin's hypothesis of development by regular choice remaining parts a foundation of organic bits of knowledge. The idea that species develop over the long run through the differential endurance and generation of creatures with favorable attributes has changed how we might interpret biodiversity. Progresses in atomic science, fossil science, and relative life structures further add to the always advancing embroidery of developmental bits of knowledge.

3. **Science: Building Blocks of Issue**
Occasional Table and Basic Bits of knowledge:

Dmitri Mendeleev's formation of the occasional table in 1869 coordinated the realized components in light of their properties, uncovering a deliberate example that underlies the variety of issue. This fundamental knowledge has worked with the forecast of unseen components as well as added to how we might interpret synthetic holding, reactivity, and the way of behaving of materials.

Nanotechnology:

The investigation of the nanoscale has prompted progressive bits of knowledge in science, physical science, and materials science. Controlling matter at the nuclear and sub-atomic levels has opened new wildernesses for planning materials with exceptional properties. Nanotechnology holds guarantee in fields going from medication and gadgets to energy and natural remediation.

4. **Cosmology: Testing the Universe**
Infinite Microwave Foundation Radiation:

The revelation of the astronomical microwave foundation radiation by Arno Penzias and Robert Wilson in 1965 gave significant proof to the Theory of the universe's origin. This weak radiation pervading the universe fills in as a depiction of the early universe, offering experiences into its starting point, development, and creation.

Exoplanets and the Quest for Extraterrestrial Life:

Progressions in adaptive innovation have empowered space experts to find huge number of exoplanets past our planetary group. The mission for tenable universes and the quest for biosignatures on far off planets address logical experiences that fuel our interest in the chance of life past Earth.

5. **Natural Science: Exploring the Anthropocene**
Environmental Change Bits of knowledge:

Logical bits of knowledge into environmental change, driven by human exercises, have raised dire worries about the strength of our planet. Figuring out the effects of ozone harming substance discharges, climbing temperatures, and changing weather conditions is fundamental for conceiving relief and transformation techniques to address the difficulties presented by a warming environment.

Biodiversity and Biological system Elements:

Investigating the mind boggling snare of life on Earth gives bits of knowledge into the significance of biodiversity for environment dependability and flexibility. Preservation science and nature add to how we might interpret the fragile equilibrium that supports life, stressing the requirement for manageable practices to protect the lavishness of our planet's organic variety.

6. **Brain research and Neuroscience: Interpreting the Psyche**

Brain adaptability:

The idea of brain adaptability, the mind's capacity to rearrange itself because of involvement, challenges prior thoughts of fixed brain structures. Experiences from brain adaptability have suggestions for learning, memory, and restoration, offering expect mediations in neurological issues and mind wounds.

Mental Experiences:

Progresses in mental brain research and neuroscience have given bits of knowledge into human cognizance, direction, and the systems hidden discernment. The investigation of cognizance, memory development, and the brain premise of feelings adds to how we might interpret the complexities of the human psyche.

7. **Software engineering: From Calculations to Man-made reasoning**

Algorithmic Experiences:

The improvement of calculations, the bit by bit systems for taking care of issues, has had significant ramifications for software engineering and different disciplines. Algorithmic bits of knowledge support the working of web search tools, information examination, and advancement issues, impacting our regular routines in manners we frequently underestimate.

Man-made consciousness and AI:

The ascent of man-made consciousness (computer based intelligence) and AI addresses a change in outlook in registering. Bits of knowledge from these fields have prompted the advancement of frameworks fit for gaining from information, perceiving examples, and simply deciding. Man-made intelligence has applications in regions as different as medical services, finance, and independent vehicles, molding the fate of innovation.

8. **Interdisciplinary Bits of knowledge: Connecting Disciplinary Limits**

Frameworks Thinking:

The acknowledgment of the interconnectedness of regular and human frameworks has brought about the field of frameworks thinking. Experiences from frameworks science assist with tending to complex difficulties by considering the communications and criticism circles that describe dynamic frameworks, offering an all encompassing way to deal with critical thinking.

Manufactured Science:

At the convergence of science and designing, engineered science looks to plan and build new natural frameworks. Experiences from this interdisciplinary field have suggestions for making manufactured creatures, designing natural circuits, and tending to difficulties in medication, energy, and ecological preservation.

7.1Research and Studies on Kangaroo Parenting

Kangaroo nurturing, otherwise called kangaroo care or skin-to-healthy skin, is a technique for holding and really focusing on infants, especially untimely newborn children, where the child is held against the parent's exposed chest. This training, propelled by the normal way of behaving of kangaroos, has earned respect for its possible advantages in advancing the prosperity of both preterm and full-term babies. In this far reaching investigation, we will dive into the broad exploration and studies directed on kangaroo nurturing, looking at the physiological, mental, and formative results related with this personal providing care approach.

1. **Authentic Setting and Development of Kangaroo Nurturing:**
   Starting points of Kangaroo Care:
   The idea of kangaroo care started during the 1970s in Bogotá, Colombia, as a reaction to the lack of hatcheries in neonatal concentrated care units (NICUs). Dr. Edgar Rey Sanabria, a Colombian pediatrician, and Dr. Hector Martinez, an obstetrician, created kangaroo care as an elective strategy to give warmth, insurance, and sustenance to untimely newborn children.
   Worldwide Reception and Transformation:
   Since its origin, kangaroo care has earned worldwide respect and has been taken on in different structures across various societies and medical services settings. The training has developed to incorporate untimely babies as well as full-term infants and newborn children with different ailments, cultivating a more comprehensive way to deal with nurturing.

2. **Physiological Advantages of Kangaroo Nurturing:**
   Temperature Guideline:
   One of the earliest noticed advantages of kangaroo care is its job in temperature guideline. Skin-to-skin contact balances out the newborn child's internal heat level, decreasing the requirement for outer warming gadgets. The glow given by the parent's chest upholds the baby's capacity to keep a steady and ideal internal heat level.
   Respiratory Soundness:
   Research shows that kangaroo care can decidedly affect respiratory soundness in untimely babies. The closeness of the parent's chest gives a consoling climate that might add to worked on respiratory examples, decreasing the rate of apnea

and bradycardia in preterm babies.

Cardiovascular Wellbeing:

Kangaroo care has been related with constructive outcomes on cardiovascular wellbeing. The quieting impact of skin-to-skin contact has been connected to further developed pulse fluctuation and improved cardiovascular dependability in untimely babies, advancing by and large heart wellbeing.

Weight Gain and Development:

Studies have shown that babies who get kangaroo care might encounter upgraded weight gain and development contrasted with the individuals who get conventional consideration. The nearby actual contact, joined with the arrival of holding chemicals like oxytocin, adds to further developed taking care of examples and dietary admission.

3. **Mental and Formative Viewpoints:**

Holding and Connection:

Kangaroo nurturing cultivates areas of strength for an of holding and connection among guardians and babies. The skin-to-skin contact advances the arrival of oxytocin, frequently alluded to as the "holding chemical," which assumes a urgent part in fostering a safe and sustaining connection between the guardian and the newborn child.

Decrease of Pressure and Uneasiness:

The quieting impact of kangaroo care stretches out to the decrease of pressure and nervousness in the two guardians and newborn children. Skin-to-skin contact has been displayed to bring down cortisol levels, a pressure chemical, advancing a more loose and soothing climate in the NICU and at home.

Neurodevelopmental Advantages:

Long haul concentrates on the effect of kangaroo care propose potential neurodevelopmental benefits for untimely newborn children. Worked on mental turn of events, tactile mix, and close to home guideline are among the noticed results, showing a positive impact on the baby's by and large neurological prosperity.

Parental Certainty and Strengthening:

Participating in kangaroo care enables guardians by giving them a substantial and dynamic job in their newborn child's consideration. This feeling of inclusion and closeness adds to expanded parental certainty, especially for those exploring the difficulties of really focusing on an untimely or restoratively delicate newborn child.

4. **Kangaroo Nurturing in Different Settings:**

NICU Settings:

Kangaroo care has turned into a standard practice in numerous NICUs around the world. Its application in the NICU setting has been related with more limited clinic stays, further developed weight gain, and improved parent-baby holding. Medical services suppliers perceive the significance of coordinating kangaroo care into the consideration plan for untimely and low-birth-weight newborn children.

Local area and Home Consideration:

Kangaroo nurturing isn't restricted to medical clinic settings. Many guardians keep on rehearsing kangaroo care at home, expanding its advantages past the NICU. This approach permits families to keep up with the nearby association laid out during the clinic stay and supports progressing formative and profound prosperity.

5. **Difficulties and Contemplations:**

Social and Social Elements:

In spite of the perceived advantages of kangaroo care, social and social elements might impact its acknowledgment and reception. In certain societies, the training might confront opposition because of customary convictions or misinterpretations. Teaching people group about the proof based benefits and dissipating fantasies is fundamental for advancing more extensive acknowledgment.

Availability to Assets:

Availability to assets and backing for kangaroo care can change. In certain locales, medical services offices might come up short on vital foundation or training projects to advance kangaroo care successfully. Tending to these inconsistencies is critical for guaranteeing that all newborn children, paying little mind to geographic area, approach the likely advantages of kangaroo nurturing.

6. **Continuous Exploration and Future Headings:**

Long haul Follow-Up Examinations:

Continuous exploration keeps on investigating the drawn out impacts of kangaroo care on the formative results of newborn children into youth and puberty. Understanding the supported effect of early skin-to-skin contact on mental, close to home, and social improvement is a critical focal point of longitudinal investigations.

Neuroscientific Examinations:

Propels in neuroimaging strategies give a chance to dig further into the neurological systems hidden the advantages of kangaroo care. Neuroscientific examinations plan to reveal the effect of skin-to-skin contact on mental health, brain network, and the foundation of fundamental mental and profound pathways.

Worldwide Execution and Promotion:

Future headings in kangaroo nurturing research include worldwide execution and backing endeavors. Guaranteeing that kangaroo care is generally perceived, acknowledged, and incorporated into neonatal consideration rehearses across different medical services frameworks stays a need. Cooperative drives can add to a more extensive comprehension of its advantages and address difficulties to execution.

7.2 Contributions to Parenting Science

Nurturing is a diverse and dynamic excursion that shapes the improvement of people from early stages through adulthood. Throughout the long term, nurturing science has arisen as an unmistakable field of study, drawing on bits of knowledge from different disciplines to investigate the intricacies of kid raising. This exposition investigates the commitments to nurturing science, analyzing the exploration, hypotheses, and systems that have improved how we might interpret the perplexing transaction between guardians, youngsters, and the more extensive socio-social setting.

1. **Authentic Advancement of Nurturing Science:**
Early Mental Speculations:
The underlying foundations of nurturing science can be followed back to early mental speculations that looked to grasp the impact of parental ways of behaving on youngster improvement. Psychoanalytic speculations, spearheaded by Sigmund Freud and Erik Erikson, underscored the job of early parent-kid connections in molding character and profound prosperity.
Behaviorism and Nurturing Practices:
The behaviorist viewpoint, promoted by B.F. Skinner, zeroed in on recognizable ways of behaving and support in parent-kid communications. Behaviorism affected nurturing science by featuring the effect of ecological boosts on molding youngsters' ways of behaving and the job of uplifting feedback in advancing positive results.

2. **Nurturing Styles and Approaches:**
Diana Baumrind's Nurturing Styles:
The fundamental work of clinician Diana Baumrind during the 1960s presented the idea of nurturing styles, classifying them into legitimate, dictator, lenient, and careless. This system laid the basis for understanding what different nurturing approaches mean for kids' turn of events, conduct, and generally prosperity.
Social Varieties in Nurturing:
Commitments to nurturing science reach out past Western-driven models. Analysts like Ruth Chao have investigated social varieties in nurturing works on, stressing the significance of understanding how different social settings shape parental assumptions, discipline procedures, and correspondence designs.

3. **Connection Hypothesis and Parent-Youngster Bonds:**
John Bowlby's Connection Hypothesis:
Connection hypothesis, created by John Bowlby, reformed how we might interpret parent-kid bonds. Bowlby's work featured the meaning of secure connections in earliest stages for close to home guideline, social turn of events, and the arrangement of relational connections all through the life expectancy.
Mary Ainsworth's Odd Circumstance:
Mary Ainsworth developed Bowlby's connection hypothesis by fostering What

is going on technique, which characterized baby parent connection designs. This examination device became instrumental in distinguishing connection styles, for example, secure, unreliable avoidant, and uncertain conflicted, giving bits of knowledge into the nature of parent-kid connections.

4. **Mental and Socio-Profound Turn of events:**
Jean Piaget's Mental Turn of events:
Jean Piaget's mental advancement hypothesis added to nurturing science by clarifying the phases of mental development in youngsters. Understanding kids' thought process, reason, and interaction data has suggestions for adjusting nurturing systems to help ideal mental turn of events.

The capacity to understand individuals at their core and Interactive abilities:
The investigation of the capacity to understand anyone on a deeper level, promoted by Daniel Goleman, has improved nurturing science by underlining the significance of cultivating close to home mindfulness and guideline in youngsters. Guardians assume a urgent part in supporting their kids' social and close to home abilities, adding to their general versatility and prosperity.

5. **Contemporary Points of view on Nurturing Science:**
Positive Nurturing and Versatility:
Positive nurturing, as advocated by analysts like Martin Seligman, centers around encouraging strength, good faith, and prosperity in youngsters. Positive nurturing systems expect to establish a strong and sustaining climate that urges youngsters to foster an inspirational perspective on life and explore difficulties really.

Parental Effects on Scholarly Accomplishment:
Research in instructive brain science plays investigated the part of parental association, assumptions, and backing in affecting kids' scholarly accomplishment. Understanding how guardians add to their youngsters' instructive encounters is fundamental for advancing effective learning results.

6. **Neuroscientific Commitments:**
Neurobiology of Nurturing:
Propels in neuroscience have given remarkable bits of knowledge into the neurobiology of nurturing. Neuroimaging studies have investigated the brain components basic parent-kid holding, profound guideline, and the effect of early encounters on mental health.

Epigenetics and Parental Impact:
Epigenetic research has revealed insight into how parental ways of behaving and ecological variables can impact quality articulation in youngsters. This field highlights the unique interaction among nature and support, underlining the enduring effect of nurturing rehearses on an organic level.

7. **Effect of Innovation and Online Entertainment:**
Advanced Nurturing and Screen Time:
The approach of innovation has presented new difficulties and amazing open doors for nurturing science. Scientists explore the effect of screen time, computerized media, and social stages on parent-kid connections, mental turn of events, and socio-close to home prosperity.
Web based Nurturing People group:
Web based nurturing networks and online entertainment stages have become spaces for guardians to share encounters, look for counsel, and structure virtual encouraging groups of people. Understanding the elements of advanced nurturing networks adds as far as anyone is concerned of how innovation shapes contemporary nurturing rehearses.

8. **Nurturing Science and Social Ability:**
Social Ability in Nurturing Exploration:
Recognizing the different social settings wherein nurturing happens is fundamental for socially equipped examination. Endeavors to consolidate social points of view in nurturing science add to a more nuanced comprehension of how social variables shape nurturing convictions, practices, and results.
Multifacetedness and Nurturing:
The multifacetedness structure, which perceives the interconnected idea of social characters and encounters, has been applied to nurturing science. Research investigating the multifacetedness of race, nationality, orientation, and financial status illuminates a more thorough comprehension regarding how numerous elements converge to shape nurturing encounters.

9. **Challenges and Moral Contemplations:**
Moral Contemplations in Nurturing Exploration:
As nurturing science progresses, moral contemplations become vital. Issues like informed assent, security, and possible mischief to members should be painstakingly addressed to guarantee that exploration contributes emphatically to the prosperity of families.
Social Responsiveness and Inclination:
The potential for social predisposition in nurturing research features the significance of social responsiveness. Specialists should endeavor to alleviate predispositions and perceive the impact of social settings on nurturing practices and results.

10. **Useful Applications and Mediations:**
Nurturing Projects and Mediations:
Nurturing science has made ready for proof based nurturing projects and mediations. These projects, like the Triple P (Positive Nurturing System) and Unbelievable Years, offer reasonable methodologies and backing to guardians, upgrading their nurturing abilities and advancing positive kid results.

Preventive Intercessions for In danger Families:
Research in nurturing science has informed preventive mediations for in danger families. Programs that target families confronting difficulties, for example, destitution, substance misuse, or emotional well-being issues expect to break the pattern of misfortune and establish a strong climate for kids.

11. **Future Bearings and Arising Subjects:**

Transdisciplinary Approaches:
The future of nurturing science includes transdisciplinary approaches that incorporate experiences from brain research, neuroscience, humanism, training, and different fields. Cooperative exploration endeavors can yield a more comprehensive comprehension of nurturing that considers the intricate interaction of organic, mental, and socio-social variables.

Nurturing in the Computerized Age:
As innovation keeps on molding the scene of nurturing, future examination will dig into the ramifications of nurturing in the computerized age. Understanding how arising innovations, computerized reasoning, and virtual encounters influence parent-kid connections will be a key concentration.

7.3 Implications for Human Child Development
Human kid improvement is a perplexing and dynamic interaction impacted by a horde of variables, going from hereditary inclinations to ecological encounters. This complete investigation dives into the ramifications for human youngster advancement, drawing experiences according to different interdisciplinary viewpoints. We will analyze the significant effect of natural, mental, social, and social variables on the various phases of kid advancement, from earliest stages through puberty. By incorporating research discoveries, speculations, and down to earth applications, this exposition means to give a comprehensive comprehension of the multifaceted excursion of human kid improvement.

1. **Natural Underpinnings of Kid Improvement:**
Hereditary qualities and Legacy:
The job of hereditary qualities in human youngster advancement couldn't possibly be more significant. Hereditary variables add to the physical, mental, and profound traits of a person. Understanding the transaction among qualities and climate is pivotal for unwinding the intricacies of hereditary effects on characteristics like insight, disposition, and helplessness to specific problems.

Mental health:
The early long periods of life are portrayed by fast mental health, establishing the groundwork for mental, close to home, and social capacities. Experiences from neuroscience feature the basic time frames during which explicit cerebrum locales go through critical development and advancement. The pliancy of the

cerebrum considers transformation and getting the hang of, stressing the significance of early encounters in molding brain connections.

Synapses and Chemicals:

Synapses and chemicals assume essential parts in controlling different parts of youngster improvement. For instance, the arrival of oxytocin, frequently alluded to as the "holding chemical," cultivates connection among parental figures and newborn children. Figuring out the neurochemical underpinnings of feelings, stress reactions, and social associations adds to bits of knowledge into human way of behaving and improvement.

2. **Mental Turn of events:**

Piaget's Phases of Mental Turn of events:

Jean Piaget's compelling hypothesis of mental improvement frames unmistakable stages through which kids progress as they develop how they might interpret the world. From the sensorimotor stage to formal functional idea, Piaget's model gives a system to grasping the developing mental capacities of kids.

Vygotsky's Sociocultural Hypothesis:

Lev Vygotsky's sociocultural hypothesis accentuates the job of social cooperations, social setting, and language in mental turn of events. The idea of the zone of proximal improvement highlights the significance of directed learning and joint effort in propelling kids' mental capacities.

Data Handling Model:

The data handling model perspectives mental advancement from the perspective of data handling capacities, including consideration, memory, and critical thinking.

Bits of knowledge according to this point of view add to how we might interpret how kids procure, store, and recover data as they explore mental undertakings.

3. **Close to home and Social Turn of events:**

Connection Hypothesis:

John Bowlby's connection hypothesis investigates the profound bonds shaped among parental figures and newborn children. Secure connections in youth add to close to home guideline, social skill, and the improvement of inward working models that shape future connections.

Erikson's Psychosocial Stages:

Erik Erikson's psychosocial progressive phases feature the interaction between individual personality and social connections. From trust versus doubt in early stages to honesty versus despair in late adulthood, Erikson's model outlines the socio-personal difficulties and achievements across the life expectancy.

Social Learning Hypothesis:

Albert Bandura's social learning hypothesis underscores the job of observational learning and demonstrating in shaping way of behaving. Kids get interactive abilities, standards, and values by noticing and copying the ways of behaving of others, building up the interconnectedness of mental and social turn of events.

4. **Language Advancement:**
Chomsky's Language Obtaining Gadget:
Noam Chomsky's hypothesis places the presence of a language securing gadget, a natural mental instrument that empowers kids to procure language quickly and easily. This viewpoint has significant ramifications for grasping the basic period for language securing and the all inclusive parts of semantic turn of events.
Sociolinguistics and Social Impacts:
Sociolinguistic viewpoints highlight the effect of social and social elements on language improvement. Various semantic conditions, language input, and social standards add to varieties in language securing designs and open styles across various networks.

5. **Moral and Moral Turn of events:**
Kohlberg's Phases of Moral Turn of events:
Lawrence Kohlberg's hypothesis of moral advancement portrays stages through which people progress in how they might interpret ethical quality. From pre-conventional profound quality to postconventional ethical quality, Kohlberg's model gives experiences into the advancing idea of moral thinking and moral direction.
Social Varieties in Virtues:
Social impacts assume a huge part in forming virtues and moral viewpoints. Multifaceted examination in moral advancement features the variety of moral systems and the effect of social standards on the arrangement of moral decisions.

6. **Relational peculiarities and Nurturing Styles:**
Baumrind's Nurturing Styles:
Diana Baumrind's arrangement of nurturing styles — definitive, tyrant, lenient, and careless — has significant ramifications for youngster improvement. The harmony among warmth and control impacts youngsters' confidence, independence, and adherence to cultural standards.
Family Frameworks Hypothesis:
The family frameworks hypothesis thinks about the family as an interconnected and related unit. Looking at relational peculiarities, correspondence examples, and job tasks adds to understanding what the family climate means for a youngster's personal and social turn of events.

7. **Instructive Ramifications:**
Instructive Brain research and Learning Hypotheses:
Bits of knowledge from instructive brain science, including behaviorism, constructivism, and socio-constructivism, illuminate educational practices and educational program plan. Understanding how kids learn, hold data, and participate in instructive settings adds to the upgrade of showing strategies and

learning results.

Comprehensive Schooling and Extraordinary Requirements:
Comprehensive schooling perceives and obliges the different requirements and capacities of youngsters. Experiences from a custom curriculum and formative brain science add to establishing comprehensive conditions that help the mental, social, and close to home improvement, everything being equal.

8. **Orientation and Character Advancement:**
Orientation Character Development:
Research in orientation and character advancement investigates how kids come to comprehend and communicate their orientation personality. The interchange of natural, social, and mental elements adds to the intricacies of orientation improvement and the arrangement of orientation jobs.

LGBTQ+ Points of view:
Understanding the encounters of LGBTQ+ kids and young people is fundamental for advancing inclusivity and supporting their character advancement. Research on LGBTQ+ nurturing, separation, and emotional well-being adds to establishing insisting conditions for assorted orientation and sexual characters.

9. **Innovation and Media Impact:**
Advanced Locals and Media Education:
Experiencing childhood in the advanced age, kids are frequently alluded to as "computerized locals." The ramifications of innovation on kid improvement, including screen time, web-based entertainment, and online connections, are subjects of progressing research. Media proficiency and computerized citizenship become fundamental parts of schooling and nurturing in the 21st hundred years.

Augmented Reality and Instructive Innovation:
Progresses in augmented simulation and instructive innovation offer new roads for improving opportunities for growth. Understanding how virtual conditions influence mental, profound, and social advancement gives important experiences to incorporating innovation into instructive practices.

10. **Ecological and Financial Variables:**
Neediness and Youngster Advancement:
Financial elements, especially neediness, have significant ramifications for kid advancement. Research features the effect of monetary differences on admittance to assets, instructive open doors, and in general prosperity, stressing the significance of tending to social imbalances.

Social Setting and Worldwide Viewpoints:
Social settings shape youngster raising practices and impact the standards and assumptions related with kid improvement. Near research across societies offers experiences into universalities and social varieties in nurturing styles, instructive practices, and socio-close to home turn of events.

11. **Psychological wellness and Prosperity:**
    Early Intercession and Avoidance:
    Early recognizable proof and mediation for psychological well-being concerns are basic for advancing positive kid advancement. Experiences from formative psychopathology illuminate preventive measures, emotional wellness advancement, and mediations pointed toward tending to mental difficulties in youth.
    Strength and Survival strategies:
    Grasping flexibility — the capacity to return from difficulty — gives experiences into defensive factors and survival strategies that cultivate positive youngster advancement. Research in flexibility adds to methodologies for advancing psychological wellness and prosperity despite challenges.
12. **Cross-Cutting Topics and Interdisciplinary Methodologies:**

Diversity in Youngster Improvement:

The diversity system recognizes the interconnected idea of social characters and encounters. Applying an interconnected focal point to kid advancement research perceives the effect of different variables, like race, orientation, and financial status, on the assorted encounters of youngsters.

Transdisciplinary Joint effort:

Interdisciplinary joint effort includes coordinating experiences from different fields to acquire a more exhaustive comprehension of human kid improvement. Joint efforts between clinicians, teachers, neuroscientists, sociologists, and different disciplines add to a comprehensive methodology that thinks about the multi-layered nature of youngster improvement.

Chapter 8

Beyond the Pouch - Growing Up Kangaroo

The kangaroo, a famous image of Australia, isn't only a magnetic marsupial known for its particular bouncing style. It likewise holds an extraordinary spot in the collective of animals because of its surprising regenerative and nurturing systems. Past the pocket, where youthful kangaroos spend their initial days, lies an interesting excursion of development and improvement. This thorough investigation dives into the existence stages, ways of behaving, and transformations that characterize growing up kangaroo. From birth to adulthood, kangaroos explore the difficulties of the Australian scene, displaying a mix of natural wonders and endurance impulses that make them an interesting subject of study.

1. **Birth and Early Days in the Pocket:**
   Birth and Size Variations:
   Kangaroos, in the same way as other marsupials, bring forth exceptionally lacking youthful. A joey, the term for a child kangaroo, is brought into the world after a moderately short development time frame and is about the size of a lima bean. The birth interaction is a perplexing interchange of impulse and maternal consideration, making way for the special excursion that follows.
   Pocket Passage and Connection:
   The pocket is an unmistakable component of marsupials, including kangaroos. The immature joey slithers into the mother's pocket, directed by a blend of nature and maternal help. When inside, the joey joins itself to one of the mother's nipples, where it goes through additional improvement in the well-being of the pocket.
   Pocket Improvement Stages:
   Inside the pocket, the joey goes through transformative phases, bit by bit acquiring strength and coordination. The mother gives sustenance and insurance, and the pocket offers a warm and get climate significant for the joey's endurance during its weak early days.

2. **Weaning and Development:**
Weaning Interaction:
As the joey keeps on developing, the weaning system starts. The progress from milk to strong food includes a continuous change in the joey's eating regimen, acquainting it with the vegetation that describes the kangaroo's herbivorous way of life. The mother's part in working with this change is a demonstration of the many-sided equilibrium of maternal consideration and normal senses.

Arising out of the Pocket:
The earth shattering event of rising up out of the pocket denotes a critical achievement in a youthful kangaroo's life. At this stage, the joey begins to wander outside the pocket, step by step expanding its openness to the outer climate. This period is vital for the advancement of coordinated abilities, socialization, and variation to life past the defensive bounds of the pocket.

Bouncing and Motion:
Bouncing is a main trait of kangaroos and an expertise they create as a component of their movement. Youthful kangaroos, or joeys, participate in energetic jumping exercises, refining their coordination and developing the fortitude required for proficient development. The change from conditional jumps to more powerful headway is an interesting part of growing up kangaroo.

3. **Socialization and Overall vibes:**
Arrangement of Crowd Design:
Kangaroos are known for their social construction, frequently framing bunches called crowds. As youthful kangaroos keep on developing, they become coordinated into the horde structure. This socialization cycle includes associations with different kangaroos, learning ordered progressions, and grasping the elements of horde life.

Job of More seasoned Kin:
In horde settings, more established kin assume a huge part in the childhood of more youthful ones. This agreeable consideration includes sharing liabilities, from insurance to mastering fundamental basic instincts. The interchange of familial securities inside the horde adds to the general social texture of kangaroo networks.

Correspondence and Vocalization:
Kangaroos convey through various vocalizations, motions, and non-verbal communication. Growing up kangaroo includes learning and dominating this perplexing arrangement of correspondence, essential for exploring social collaborations, laying out pecking orders, and flagging expected dangers.

4. **Exploring the Australian Scene:**
Scavenging Conduct:
As youthful kangaroos mature, they effectively take part in scrounging exercises. The Australian scene, with its different vegetation, becomes both a jungle gym

and a wellspring of food. Understanding the scavenging conduct of youthful kangaroos gives bits of knowledge into their dietary inclinations, nourishing requirements, and variation to differing natural circumstances.

Water Reliance and Variations:

Kangaroos are very much adjusted to Australia's dry scene, and water is a basic asset for their endurance. Youthful kangaroos, specifically, figure out how to explore the difficulties of water shortage, creating methodologies for productive hydration and adjusting to the variable accessibility of water sources.

Movement and Investigation:

Kangaroos are known for their traveling way of life, and growing up includes learning the specialty of movement and investigation. Youthful kangaroos, directed by their inborn impulses and affected by the ways of behaving of more established individuals in the horde, participate in occasional developments to track down food, water, and reasonable living spaces.

5. **Conceptive Development and Being a parent:**

Conceptive Turn of events:

As youthful kangaroos arrive at conceptive development, they become dynamic members in the propagation of their species. Understanding the regenerative improvement of kangaroos reveals insight into the complexities of romance, mating ceremonies, and the job of chemicals in setting off conceptive ways of behaving.

Mating Methodologies and Social Elements:

Kangaroos display special mating methodologies, with predominant guys vieing for the consideration of females. Noticing the social elements of mating customs gives bits of knowledge into the complicated order inside kangaroo crowds and the manners by which rivalry and collaboration coincide.

Joey Care and Parental Jobs:

Being a parent is a recurrent cycle in kangaroo life. Youthful females, having arrived at conceptive development, become moms, while more seasoned ages take on grandparental jobs. Figuring out the repetitive idea of kangaroo being a parent, with progressive ages adding to the endurance of the crowd, adds profundity to our enthusiasm for their social design.

6. **Difficulties and Variations:**

Hunter Evasion and Guard Systems:

Growing up kangaroo isn't without its difficulties, and hunter evasion is a basic part of endurance. Youthful kangaroos figure out how to perceive likely dangers and utilize protection systems, for example, jumping, boxing with their strong rear legs, and looking for asylum in the wellbeing of the crowd.

Natural Tensions and Versatility:

The Australian climate presents a scope of difficulties, from outrageous temperatures to food shortage. Youthful kangaroos show versatility by creating physiological and conduct systems to adapt to these ecological tensions. Understanding how kangaroos explore these difficulties adds to our enthusiasm for their strength.

Human-Untamed life Association:

Human-untamed life cooperation represents a special arrangement of difficulties for kangaroos. As urbanization infringes on normal living spaces, youthful kangaroos should adjust to human presence, explore metropolitan scenes, and fight with possible contentions. Investigating the elements of human-kangaroo communication reveals insight into protection endeavors and concurrence techniques.

7. **Preservation and Environmental Importance:**

Job in Environments:

Kangaroos assume a crucial part in Australian environments as herbivores, impacting vegetation elements and adding to supplement cycling. The biological meaning of kangaroos stretches out past their alluring appearance, making them vital parts of the multifaceted trap of life in Australia.

Preservation Difficulties:

In spite of their biological significance, kangaroos face preservation challenges. Understanding the effect of variables, for example, environment misfortune, environmental change, and human exercises on kangaroo populaces adds to preservation endeavors pointed toward guaranteeing the drawn out reasonability of these famous marsupials.

Protection Drives:

Protection drives center around saving kangaroo living spaces, relieving human-natural life clashes, and executing maintainable administration rehearses. Investigating these drives gives bits of knowledge into the cooperative endeavors of scientists, protectionists, and nearby networks to defend the fate of kangaroo populaces.

8. **Social Importance and Imagery:**

Native Viewpoints:

Kangaroos hold social importance in Native Australian people group. They highlight unmistakably in Dreamtime stories, workmanship, and conventional practices. Understanding the social viewpoints and imagery related with kangaroos improves our enthusiasm for their part in Native legacy.

Public Imagery:

Kangaroos are significant of Australia as well as act as an image of public character. They are highlighted on the nation's emblem and are broadly perceived as a notorious portrayal of the special natural life that occupies the Australian mainland.

9. **Logical Exploration and Revelations:**

Mechanical Progressions in Kangaroo Exploration:

Logical exploration on kangaroos has profited from innovative progressions, including GPS following, satellite symbolism, and hereditary investigation. These devices empower scientists to assemble complete information on kangaroo conduct, developments, and populace elements, adding to a more profound comprehension of their biology.

Commitments to Similar Science:

Kangaroos offer interesting experiences into similar science, especially in regards to marsupial conceptive techniques, movement, and variations to parched conditions. Similar examinations including kangaroos add to how we might interpret mammalian development and the variety of life history procedures in the collective of animals.

8.1Gradual Transition from Pouch to Independence

In the collective of animals, marsupials stand apart for their special regenerative procedure, portrayed by the introduction of exceptionally lacking youthful that proceed with their improvement in a pocket. This exposition dives into the entrancing universe of marsupial turn of events, zeroing in on the steady change from pocket to freedom. From birth to weaning, marsupials explore a mind boggling venture that includes versatile ways of behaving, maternal consideration, and the procurement of abilities fundamental for endurance. While the kangaroo fills in as an essential model, experiences from different marsupials add to a complete comprehension of this phenomenal formative cycle.

1. **Birth and Beginning Maternal Consideration:**
   Precocial versus Altricial Birth:
   Marsupials display a scope of formative techniques, from the somewhat precocial youthful of bandicoots to the profoundly altricial youthful of kangaroos and opossums. Understanding the varieties in birth procedures makes way for investigating the assorted manners by which marsupials progress from pocket subordinate babies to free adolescents.

   Maternal Licking and Preparing:
   Maternal consideration is an essential part of marsupial turn of events, beginning from the snapshot of birth. Moms take part in licking and prepping ways of behaving to animate their young and work with their excursion to the pocket. This underlying consideration sets the establishment for the nearby connection between marsupial moms and their posterity.

   Creeping to the Pocket:
   The excursion from the birth trench to the pocket is an exceptional accomplishment for marsupial youthful. Their immature state expects them to slither independent to the wellbeing of the pocket, directed by a mix of nature and the material signals given by the mother. This excursion is a basic move toward the progressive change from weakness to security.

2. **Pocket Improvement Stages:**
Sustenance and Connection:
The pocket fills in as a defensive climate where marsupial youthful proceed with their turn of events. Inside the pocket, connection to a nipple gives sustenance, fundamental for development and endurance. Understanding the progressive phases inside the pocket reveals insight into the interesting transformations that marsupials have advanced.

Weaning Interaction:
Weaning in marsupials is a slow cycle, unmistakable from the unexpected weaning saw in numerous placental well evolved creatures. The pocket gives a protected space to youthful marsupials to progress from milk to strong food. The progressive presentation of strong food into their eating routine lines up with their formative necessities and status.

3. **Rising up out of the Pocket:**
Exploratory Way of behaving:
The progress from pocket to autonomy includes exploratory way of behaving. Youthful marsupials start to wander outside the pocket, steadily expanding their reach and communicating with the outer climate. This exploratory stage is significant for the procurement of tangible and coordinated abilities essential for endurance.

Jumping and Velocity:
In species like kangaroos, jumping is an unmistakable method of headway. The slow improvement of bouncing abilities is an intriguing part of the progress to freedom. Seeing how youthful marsupials refine their abilities to bounce gives bits of knowledge into the coordination, strength, and versatility expected for proficient development.

Socialization with Kin:
Numerous marsupials, particularly those that structure gatherings, participate in socialization with kin. Communications with peers add to the improvement of interactive abilities, collaboration, and the foundation of progressive systems inside the gathering. Kin elements assume a huge part in the progress to freedom.

4. **Acquiring Basic instincts:**
Searching and Dietary Transformations:
The slow progress to autonomy includes mastering fundamental basic instincts, including rummaging and dietary variations. Youthful marsupials figure out how to distinguish reasonable food sources, separate among eatable and non-consumable things, and adjust their eating regimen to changing natural circum-stances.

Hunter Aversion Procedures:
Endurance in the wild requires powerful hunter aversion procedures. Youthful

marsupials foster techniques like stowing away, staying unmoving, or using their special motion styles to dodge expected dangers. Understanding these versatile ways of behaving adds to our enthusiasm for their part in the environment.

Natural Route:

Exploring the differed scenes of their environments is an expertise youthful marsupials procure during the progress to freedom. Understanding how they adjust to assorted landscapes, from thick timberlands to open fields, gives bits of knowledge into their natural mindfulness and capacity to flourish in various environmental specialties.

5. **Maternal Impact and Direction:**

Maternal Educating and Shows:

Maternal impact stays a directing power even as youthful marsupials become more free. Moms assume a part in showing abilities to survive, including hunting, preparing, and correspondence. Maternal exhibitions and communications add to the exchange of information essential for the posterity's prosperity.

Job of Fathers and More seasoned Kin:

In a few marsupial animal varieties, fathers and more seasoned kin likewise assume parts in directing the youthful during their progress to freedom. Helpful consideration inside marsupial families grandstands the interconnectedness of ages and the cooperative exertion engaged with guaranteeing the endurance of the species.

6. **Social Construction and Overall vibes:**

Arrangement of Gatherings:

Social construction changes among marsupials, for certain species shaping very close family gatherings or hordes. The progress to freedom includes coordination into these gatherings, where youthful marsupials gain proficiency with the subtleties of gathering residing, social orders, and helpful ways of behaving.

Correspondence and Vocalization:

Successful correspondence is fundamental for social living. Youthful marsupials foster vocalization abilities, utilizing various calls and motions toward speak with their moms, kin, and different individuals from the gathering. Understanding marsupial correspondence adds to bits of knowledge into their perplexing social elements.

7. **Conceptive Development and Life as a parent:**

Conceptive Development:

The progress to conceptive development denotes a huge stage in the existence of marsupials. Understanding the physiological and conduct changes related with regenerative development gives experiences into the continuation of the existence cycle and the propagation of the species.

Parental Jobs and Recurrent Being a parent:

Marsupials frequently show repeating being a parent, where progressive ages add to the endurance of the species. More seasoned ages take on parental jobs, directing the youthful through their change to autonomy, while the cycle go on with the introduction of new posterity.

8. **Difficulties and Transformations:**
Ecological Difficulties:
Marsupials face a scope of ecological difficulties, from climatic changes to living space modifications. The capacity of youthful marsupials to adjust to changing ecological circumstances is a demonstration of their versatility and the adaptability of their formative techniques.

Human-Natural life Communications:
Human-natural life communications present remarkable difficulties for marsupials. Urbanization, living space discontinuity, and experiences with human foundation influence the capacity of youthful marsupials to explore their surroundings. Preservation endeavors should consider these difficulties to guarantee the prosperity of marsupial populaces.

9. **Protection and Biological Importance:**
Job in Biological systems:
The biological meaning of marsupials reaches out past their formative process. As herbivores, insectivores, or omnivores, they assume critical parts in biological system elements, impacting vegetation, controlling bug populaces, and adding to supplement cycling.

Preservation Methodologies:
Marsupials face preservation challenges because of natural surroundings misfortune, environmental change, and human exercises. Powerful protection systems include safeguarding normal environments, carrying out reasonable land the board practices, and bringing issues to light about the significance of marsupials in keeping up with biological equilibrium.

10. **Near Investigations and Transformative Importance:**

Near Formative Science:
Marsupials offer novel open doors for near formative science. Concentrating on the varieties in formative methodologies among marsupials adds to how we might interpret mammalian advancement, life history systems, and the versatile variety inside the collective of animals.

Developmental Importance:
The progressive change from pocket to autonomy mirrors the transformative meaning of marsupials. Their regenerative and formative variations grandstand the adaptability of mammalian procedures for endurance and multiplication, offering significant bits of knowledge into the more extensive setting of vertebrate advancement.

8.2 Life Outside the Pouch - Socialization and Integration

The progress from pocket to freedom denotes a pivotal stage in the existence of marsupials, making way for socialization and joining into their particular surroundings. In contrast to placental warm blooded animals, marsupials, with their exceptional regenerative technique, go through early advancement in the wellbeing of the pocket. When they arise, youthful marsupials participate in a progression of social communications, mastering fundamental abilities and exploring the intricacies of their living spaces. This investigation digs into the intriguing universe of life outside the pocket, zeroing in on the socialization and combination processes that characterize the existences of marsupials across different species.

1. **Arising out of the Pocket:**
   Basic Formative Achievement:
   The rising up out of the pocket is a basic formative achievement in the existence of a marsupial. Whether it's a kangaroo joey, a koala fledgling, or a wallaby, the change to freedom includes leaving the solid limits of the pocket and entering a world loaded with difficulties and open doors.

   Exploratory Way of behaving:
   Arising out of the pocket denotes the start of exploratory way of behaving. Youthful marsupials, directed by impulse, continuously adventure into the outer climate. This stage is fundamental for creating tangible and coordinated abilities, as well concerning adjusting to the complicated world past the pocket.

   Maternal Direction:
   Maternal direction assumes a vital part during the underlying phases of development. Moms give insurance, direction, and backing as their young ones move into the rest of the world. This collaboration lays out an establishment for the connection among moms and their posterity, which stays imperative all through the beginning phases of freedom.

2. **Social Elements and Gathering Living:**
   Development of Gatherings:
   Numerous marsupials are social creatures that structure bunches for shared benefit. Gatherings, known as crowds or troops, give potential open doors to communication, collaboration, and shared assets. Understanding the development and elements of these gatherings is vital to disentangling the intricacies of marsupial socialization.

   Kin Connections:
   Kin cooperations are a typical component among marsupials. Youthful marsupials frequently include kin inside a similar litter, and these communications add to the improvement of interactive abilities. Kin play and take part in helpful ways of behaving, cultivating a feeling of friendship and shared opportunities for growth.

   Ordered progressions and Social Designs:

Marsupial social designs include ordered progressions, with prevailing and subordinate people. These ordered progressions are laid out through different ways of behaving, for example, predominance shows, preparing customs, and spatial situating inside the gathering. Understanding the subtleties of social designs gives experiences into the association of marsupial networks.

3. **Correspondence and Vocalization:**

Correspondence inside Gatherings:

Correspondence is vital to the social texture of marsupial networks. Through a blend of vocalizations, non-verbal communication, and fragrance checking, marsupials pass on data about their goals, feelings, and the climate. Noticing correspondence inside gatherings offers a brief look into the modern ways marsupials interface.

Maternal-Posterity Correspondence:

Maternal-posterity correspondence is a particular type of cooperation vital for the endurance and prosperity of youthful marsupials. Vocalizations and explicit ways of behaving among moms and their posterity work with holding, give solace, and pass fundamental data related on to somewhere safe and secure and route.

Regional Checking and Flagging:

Marsupials frequently participate in regional ways of behaving, denoting their domains with aroma organs and vocal signs. Understanding these regional elements is fundamental for grasping the social cooperations, asset dissemination, and reproducing systems inside marsupial networks.

4. **Mastering Basic instincts:**

Scrounging and Dietary Learning:

Mastering basic instincts is a constant interaction for youthful marsupials outside the pocket. Scrounging ways of behaving, including the recognizable proof of appropriate food sources and the improvement of taking care of procedures, are vital for their healthful prosperity. Learning dietary inclinations and variations guarantees their capacity to explore fluctuated biological systems.

Hunter Evasion Techniques:

The outside climate opens marsupials to possible hunters. Youthful marsupials learn hunter aversion systems, for example, perceiving peril signals, looking for asylum in safe areas, and utilizing one of a kind motion styles for dodging dangers. The procurement of these abilities is fundamental for their endurance in nature.

Natural Route:

Exploring the different scenes of their environments is an expertise youthful marsupials gain during the beginning phases of freedom. Understanding how they adjust to different landscapes, including timberlands, meadows, and rough regions, gives bits of knowledge into their natural mindfulness and capacity to flourish in various biological specialties.

5. **Parental Impact and Helpful Consideration:**
Maternal and Fatherly Jobs:

While maternal consideration is transcendent in marsupials, a few animal varieties display helpful consideration including the two guardians. The jobs of moms and fathers fluctuate across species, for certain dads effectively partaking in safeguarding, prepping, and directing their young. Helpful consideration adds to the general prosperity of the posterity.

Kin Participation:

Kin participation is an eminent part of marsupial relational intricacies. More seasoned kin frequently assume a part in directing and safeguarding more youthful ones. This helpful consideration not just upgrades the endurance chances of the posterity yet in addition cultivates a feeling of familial bonds inside the gathering.

6. **Difficulties and Variations:**
Natural Difficulties:

Life outside the pocket opens marsupials to a bunch of ecological difficulties. These difficulties might remember changes for weather conditions, accessibility of food and water, and experiences with expected dangers. The capacity of youthful marsupials to adjust to these difficulties mirrors their flexibility and the viability of their learned methods for surviving.

Human-Natural life Association:

Human-natural life association presents interesting difficulties for marsupials. Urbanization, environment obliteration, and experiences with human framework can upset regular ways of behaving and route designs.

Understanding these difficulties is fundamental for creating preservation techniques that advance conjunction and limit human effect on marsupial populaces.

7. **Regenerative Development and Continuation of Social Elements:**
Regenerative Development:

The change from pre-adulthood to regenerative development denotes one more huge stage in the existences of marsupials. Understanding the physiological changes and ways of behaving related with conceptive development gives bits of knowledge into the continuation of social elements and the propagation of marsupial networks.

Job in Friendly Designs:

Conceptive development frequently compares with explicit jobs inside friendly designs. Predominant people might take on rearing liabilities, while more youthful individuals add to agreeable consideration and gathering exercises. The interaction between conceptive development and social jobs shapes the general working of marsupial networks.

8. **Protection and Biological Importance:**

Job in Biological systems:

Marsupials assume fundamental parts in environments as herbivores, insectivores, or omnivores. Their searching exercises, regional ways of behaving, and communications with different species add to the equilibrium of biological systems. Perceiving their natural importance is significant for forming viable preservation methodologies.

Preservation Difficulties:

Protection challenges for marsupials incorporate living space misfortune, environmental change, and human exercises. Understanding the particular social ways of behaving, route designs, and environmental necessities of various marsupial species illuminates protection endeavors. Methodologies ought to intend to save regular environments, alleviate human-natural life clashes, and advance maintainable land the executives rehearses.

9. **Relative Investigations and Logical Commitments:**

Relative Social Way of behaving:

Relative examinations across various marsupial species uncover varieties in friendly ways of behaving. Understanding these distinctions gives significant bits of knowledge into the variables molding social elements, correspondence techniques, and agreeable ways of behaving inside marsupial networks.

Commitment to Conduct Biology:

Marsupials contribute fundamentally to the field of conduct environment. Noticing their socialization processes, learning ways of behaving, and cooperations with the climate illuminates more extensive conversations on versatile procedures, conduct development, and the interconnectedness of biological frameworks.

8.3 Comparisons with Human Adolescence

While people and marsupials have a place with various parts of the mammalian tree, charming equals can be drawn between the formative phases of human youth and the development cycle saw in marsupials. Notwithstanding the immense natural contrasts, investigating these correlations reveals insight into the variety of developmental techniques because of ecological difficulties and the common significance of immaturity as a basic time of development and transformation.

Rise and Autonomy:

In the two people and marsupials, pre-adulthood denotes a huge period of arising freedom. Human youths go through a course of expanding independence, looking to lay out their personality and explore the intricacies of the social world. Likewise, marsupials, in the wake of rising up out of the pocket, leave on an excursion of investigation, leveling up their endurance abilities and bit by bit acquiring freedom inside their environments.

Socialization and Collective vibes:

Socialization is a crucial part of youth in the two people and marsupials. Human youths take part in friendly collaborations, shaping companion gatherings and exploring the complexities of cultural standards. Marsupials, especially those that show social ways of behaving, go through a comparative course of coordinating into gatherings, learning correspondence systems, and laying out pecking orders inside their networks.

Acquiring Abilities to survive:

Youthfulness fills in as a time of mastering fundamental abilities to survive in the two people and marsupials. Human young people get mental, profound, and useful abilities important for adulthood, including navigation, critical thinking, and adapting to difficulties. Essentially, youthful marsupials outside the pocket go through a period of mastering basic instincts, like scrounging, hunter evasion, and natural route, adding to their independence.

Parental Impact and Direction:

The job of parental direction stays significant during youth, whether in people or marsupials. In people, guardians offer close to home help, direction on life decisions, and a security net for investigation. In marsupials, moms and, in certain species, fathers add to the childhood of their young, offering direction, security, and fundamental abilities important for endurance in nature.

Regenerative Development:

Pre-adulthood is characteristically connected to the beginning of conceptive development, a common component among people and marsupials. Both experience hormonal changes and physiological improvements that mark the progress to regenerative adulthood. The meaning of this stage lies in the continuation of the existence cycle and the propagation of their separate species.

Difficulties and Transformations:

Youth is a time of confronting and adjusting to difficulties in both human and marsupial turn of events. Human young people battle with prevailing difficulties, scholastic difficulties, and character development. Marsupials, presented to the wild, explore ecological difficulties, learn hunter evasion methods, and adjust to variances in food accessibility and environment. The capacity to adjust during puberty contributes essentially to long haul step by step processes for surviving.

Near Social Biology:

Near examinations between human youthfulness and the development cycle in marsupials add to the more extensive field of social nature. By looking at likenesses and contrasts, researchers gain bits of knowledge into the versatile methodologies and transformative tensions that have formed the different formative pathways in warm blooded animals.